The Yale Shakespeare.

◄◄◄◄◄◄◄◄◄◄◄◄◄◄◄◄◄◄►►►►►►►►►►►►►►►►►►►

THE TRAGEDY OF OTHELLO

NEW EDITION REVISED BY

TUCKER BROOKE

PUBLISHED ON THE FUND
GIVEN TO THE YALE UNIVERSITY PRESS IN 1917
BY THE MEMBERS OF THE
KINGSLEY TRUST ASSOCIATION
(SCROLL AND KEY SOCIETY OF YALE COLLEGE)
TO COMMEMORATE THE SEVENTY-FIFTH ANNIVERSARY
OF THE FOUNDING OF THE SOCIETY

This new edition of Othello and a number of other plays in THE YALE SHAKESPEARE has been prepared by TUCKER BROOKE who has used, added to, and brought up to date the work of the previous editors whose names appear with his in the separate volumes.

The Yale Shakespeare.

The Tragedy of Othello
The Moor of Venice

EDITED BY TUCKER BROOKE

AND

LAWRENCE MASON

New Haven · Yale University Press
LONDON · GEOFFREY CUMBERLEGE
OXFORD UNIVERSITY PRESS

CONTENTS

The facsimile opposite represents the title-page of the Elizabethan Club copy of the first quarto edition. Nineteen copies of this edition are known to survive.

On the leaf following the title (A2) the publisher has introduced the following note:

THE STATIONER TO THE READER.

To set forth a booke without an Epistle, were like to the old English prouerbe, A blew coat without a badge, & the Author being dead, I thought good to take that piece of worke upon mee: To commend it, I will not, for that which is good, I hope euery man will commend, without intreaty: and I am the bolder, because the Authors name is sufficient to vent his worke. Thus leauing euery one to the liberty of iudgement: I haue ventered to print this Play, and leaue it to the generall censure.

Yours,

Thomas VValkley.

THE
Tragœdy of Othello,

The Moore of Venice.

As it hath beene diuerse times acted at the Globe, and at the Black-Friers, by his Maiesties Seruants.

Written by VVilliam Shakespeare.

LONDON,
Printed by *N. O.* for *Thomas Walkley,* and are to be sold at his shop, at the Eagle and Child, in Brittans Burſſe.
1622.

[THE ACTORS' NAMES

OTHELLO, *the Moor.*

BRABANTIO, *Father to Desdemona.*

CASSIO, *an honorable Lieutenant.*

IAGO, *a villain* ['ancient' *or standard-bearer, and third in command to Othello*].

RODERIGO, *a gulled gentleman.*

DUKE OF VENICE.

Senators.

MONTANO, *Governor of Cyprus.*

Gentlemen of Cyprus.

LODOVICO *and* ⎱ *two noble Venetians* [*kinsman and*
GRATIANO ⎰ *brother, respectively, to Brabantio*].

Sailors.

Clown [*in Othello's retinue*].

DESDEMONA, *wife to Othello* [*and daughter to Brabantio*].

EMILIA, *wife to Iago.*

BIANCA, *a courtesan.*

[*Messengers, Herald, Officers, Musicians, and Attendants*
SCENE: *Act I, at Venice; Acts II-V, at a sea-port (Famagosta) in Cyprus.*]

The Tragedy of
Othello, the Moor of Venice

ACT FIRST

SCENE FIRST

[Venice. A Street]

Enter Roderigo and Iago.

Rod. Tush! Never tell me! I take it much unkindly
That thou, Iago, who hast had my purse
As if the strings were thine, shouldst know of this.

Iago. 'Sblood, but you will not hear me!   4
If ever I did dream of such a matter,
Abhor me.

Rod. Thou told'st me thou didst hold him in thy hate.

Iago. Despise me if I do not. Three great ones of the
city,   8
In personal suit to make me his lieutenant,
Off-capp'd to him; and, by the faith of man
(I know my price), I am worth no worse a place.
But he, as loving his own pride and purposes,   12
Evades them with a bombast circumstance
Horribly stuff'd with epithets of war;
«And, in conclusion,»

---

4 'Sblood; *cf. n.*
5 matter: *i.e., the marriage of Othello and Desdemona*
8 Three great ones; *cf. n.*
10 Off-capp'd: *doffed their caps*   11 price: *value*
13 bombast circumstance: *inflated circumlocution; cf. n.*
15 *Not in Folio; see 'Textual Note'*

Nonsuits my mediators; for, 'Certes,' says he,   16
'I have already chose my officer.'
And what was he?
Forsooth, a great arithmetician,
One Michael Cassio, a Florentine   20
(A fellow almost damn'd in a fair wife),
That never set a squadron in the field,
Nor the division of a battle knows
More than a spinster,—unless the bookish theoric,   24
Wherein the toged consuls can propose
As masterly as he. Mere prattle, without practice,
Is all his soldiership; but he, sir, had the election,
And I (of whom his eyes had seen the proof   28
At Rhodes, at Cyprus, and on other grounds
Christian and heathen) must be be-lee'd and calm'd
By Debitor-and-Creditor. This counter-caster,
He, in good time, must his lieutenant be,   32
And I—God bless the mark!—his Moorship's ancient.

    Rod. By heaven, I rather would have been his hangman.
    Iago. Why, there's no remedy. 'Tis the curse of service.
Preferment goes by letter and affection,   36
And not by old gradation, where each second

16 Nonsuits: *rebuffs*   Certes: *positively*
20 Florentine; *cf. n.*   21 *Cf. n.*
23 division . . . battle: *disposition of a battle-line*
24 unless: *except, unless you count*   bookish theoric: *book-taught theory*
25 toged consuls: *councillors in their togas or robes of peace* propose: *converse, discourse*
27 election: *appointment*   30 be-lee'd and calm'd; *cf. n.*
31 *Cf. n.*   32 in good time: *(phrase of contempt)* forsooth
33 God . . . mark; *cf. n.*   ancient: *ensign; cf. n.*
36 letter: *commendatory letter, influence*   affection: *favoritism*
37 old gradation: *the old order of seniority*

Stood heir to the first. Now, sir, be judge yourself,
Whether I in any just term am affin'd
To love the Moor.

   Rod.   I would not follow him then.   40

   Iago. O sir, content you.

I follow him to serve my turn upon him;
We cannot be all masters, nor all masters
Cannot be truly follow'd. You shall mark   44
Many a duteous and knee-crooking knave,
That (doting on his own obsequious bondage)
Wears out his time much like his master's ass,
For nought but provender, and when he's old,—cashier'd!
Whip me such honest knaves. Others there are   49
Who, trimm'd in forms and visages of duty,
Keep yet their hearts attending on themselves,
And throwing but shows of service on their lords,   52
Do well thrive by 'em, and when they have lin'd their
    coats
Do themselves homage. Those fellows have some soul,
And such a one do I profess myself. For, sir,
It is as sure as you are Roderigo,   56
Were I the Moor, I would not be Iago.
In following him, I follow but myself;
Heaven is my judge, not I for love and duty,
But seeming so for my peculiar end.   60
For when my outward action does demónstrate

39 in any . . . affin'd; *cf. n.*
42 to serve . . . him: *to use him for my own advantage*
49 Whip me, *etc.: i.e., I think they should be whipped*
50 visages: *outward semblances*
53 lin'd their coats: *filled their pockets*
59 not I: *i.e., I do not do it*
60 seeming so: *seeming loving and dutiful*   peculiar: *private*

The native act and figure of my heart
In complement extern, 'tis not long after
But I will wear my heart upon my sleeve   64
For daws to peck at. I am not what I am.

Rod. What a full fortune does the thick-lips owe,
If he can carry 't thus!

Iago.   Call up her father.
Rouse him, make after him, poison his delight,   68
Proclaim him in the street, incense her kinsmen,
And though he in a fertile climate dwell,
Plague him with flies; though that his joy be joy,
Yet throw such chances of vexation on't   72
As it may lose some color.

Rod. Here is her father's house. I'll call aloud.

Iago. Do; with like timorous accent and dire yell
As when (by night and negligence) the fire   76
Is spied in populous cities.

Rod. What, ho, Brabantio! Signior Brabantio, ho!

Iago. Awake! what, ho, Brabantio! thieves! thieves!
    thieves!
Look to your house, your daughter, and your bags! 80
Thieves! thieves!

Brabantio at a window, above.

Bra. What is the reason of this terrible summons?
What is the matter there?

62 native act: *innate operation*   figure: *configuration*
63 complement extern: *outward counterpart*   'tis . . . But:
    'twill not be long before
66 owe: *possess*   67 carry't: *get away with it*
68 Rouse him; *cf. n.*
72 chances of vexation: *vexatious accidents*   73 As: *that*
76 by night and negligence: *amid nocturnal repose*

Rod. Signior, is all your family within? 84

Iago. Are your doors lock'd?

Bra. Why, wherefore ask you this?

Iago. 'Zounds, sir, you're robb'd!—For shame, put on
your gown!—

Your heart is burst, you have lost half your soul.

Even now, now, very now, an old black ram 88

Is tupping your white ewe. Arise, arise!

Awake the snorting citizens with the bell,

Or else the devil will make a grandsire of you.

Arise, I say.

Bra. What! have you lost your wits? 92

Rod. Most reverend signior, do you know my voice?

Bra. Not I. What are you?

Rod. My name is Roderigo.

Bra. The worser welcome!

I have charg'd thee not to haunt about my doors. 96

In honest plainness thou hast heard me say

My daughter is not for thee; and now, in madness,

Being full of supper and distempering draughts,

Upon malicious bravery dost thou come 100

To start my quiet.

Rod. Sir, sir, sir!

Bra. But thou must needs be sure,

My spirit and my place have in them power

To make this bitter to thee.

Rod. Patience, good sir. 104

Bra. What tell'st thou me of robbing? This is Venice.

My house is not a grange.

---

86 For shame . . . gown; *cf. n.*   90 snorting: *snoring*
100 bravery: *bravado*   101 start: *disturb*
106 grange: *lonely farmhouse*

Rod.   Most grave Brabantio,
In simple and pure soul I come to you.   107

    Iago. 'Zounds, sir, you are one of those that will
not serve God if the devil bid you. Because we come
to do you service and you think we are ruffians, you'll
have your daughter covered with a Barbary horse;
you'll have your nephews neigh to you; you'll have
coursers for cousins and gennets for germans.   113

    Bra. What profane wretch art thou?

    Iago. I am one, sir, that come to tell you, your
daughter and the Moor are now making the beast
with two backs.   117

    Bra. Thou art a villain.

    Iago.   You are—a senator.

    Bra. This thou shalt answer. I know thee, Roderigo.

    Rod. Sir, I will answer anything. But, I beseech
you,   120
⟨If 't be your pleasure and most wise consent
⟨As partly, I find, it is⟩ that your fair daughter,
At this odd-even and dull watch o' th' night,
Transported with no worse nor better guard   124
But with a knave of common hire, a góndolier,
To the gross clasps of a lascivious Moor—
If this be known to you, and your allowance,
We then have done you bold and saucy wrongs.   128
But if you know not this, my manners tell me
We have your wrong rebuke. Do not believe

112 nephews: *grandchildren*
113 coursers: *swift and spirited horses*   gennets: *small Span-*
   ish horses   germans: *near relatives*
115–117 Cf. *n.*   118 a senator; *cf. n.*
121–137 *Not in Quarto; see 'Textual Note'*   123 Cf. *n.*
127 your allowance: *what you approve of*

That, from the sense of all civility,
I thus would play and trifle with your reverence.   132
Your daughter (if you have not given her leave,
I say again) hath made a gross revolt,
Tying her duty, beauty, wit and fortunes
In an extravagant and wheeling stranger   136
Of here and everywhere. Straight satisfy yourself.)
If she be in her chamber or your house,
Let loose on me the justice of the state
For thus deluding you.

Bra.   Strike on the tinder, ho!   140
Give me a taper! call up all my people!
This accident is not unlike my dream.
Belief of it oppresses me already.
Light, I say! light!   *Exit.*

Iago.   Farewell, for I must leave you.   144
It seems not meet nor wholesome to my place
To be produc'd (as, if I stay, I shall)
Against the Moor; for I do know the state
(However this may gall him with some check)   148
Cannot with safety cast him; for he's embark'd
With such loud reason to the Cyprus wars,
Which even now stand in act, that, for their souls,
Another of his fathom they have not   152
To lead their business. In which regard,
Though I do hate him as I do hell's pains,

131 from . . . all: *deprived of all regard for*
136 extravagant and wheeling: *vagabond and itinerant; cf. n.*
146 produc'd: *brought forward as witness*   148 check: *rebuke*
149 cast: *dismiss*   embark'd: *engaged, committed*
150 loud reason: *pressing necessity*   Cyprus wars; *cf. n.*
151 stand in act: *are actually under way*
152 fathom: *capacity*

Yet for necessity of present life,
I must show out a flag and sign of love,   156
Which is indeed but sign. That you shall surely find him,
Lead to the Sagittary the raised search,
And there will I be with him. So, farewell.   *Exit.*

*Enter [below] Brabantio in his night gown, and Servants
with torches.*

   Bra. It is too true an evil. Gone she is,   160
And what's to come of my despised time
Is nought but bitterness. Now, Roderigo,
Where didst thou see her? O unhappy girl!
With the Moor, sayst thou? Who would be a father!   164
How didst thou know 'twas she? O, she deceives me
Past thought. What said she to you? Get mo tapers!
Raise all my kindred! Are they married, think you?
   Rod. Truly, I think they are.   168
   Bra. O heaven! How got she out? O treason of the blood!
Fathers, from hence trust not your daughters' minds
By what you see them act. Is there not charms
By which the property of youth and maidhood   172
May be abus'd? Have you not read, Roderigo,
Of some such thing?
   Rod.   Yes, sir, I have indeed.
   Bra. Call up my brother. O, would you had had her!
Some one way, some another! Do you know   176
Where we may apprehend her and the Moor?

158 Sagittary: *an inn; cf. n.*
159 S.d. night gown: *dressing robe*
161 what's . . . time: *the remainder of my wretched life*
163 unhappy; *cf. n.*
166 mo: *more*
172 property: *nature*   175 brother: *i.e., Gratiano*

Rod. I think I can discover him, if you please
To get good guard and go along with me.

    Bra. Pray, lead me on. At every house I'll call;   180
I may command at most. Get weapons, ho!
And raise some special officers of night.
On, good Roderigo. I'll deserve your pains.   *Exeunt.*

SCENE SECOND

[Another Street. Before the Sagittary]

Enter Othello, Iago, and Attendants with torches.

    Iago. Though in the trade of war I have slain men,
Yet do I hold it very stuff o' th' conscience
To do no contriv'd murder. I lack iniquity
Sometimes to do me service. Nine or ten times   4
I had thought t' have yerk'd him here under the ribs.

    Oth. 'Tis better as it is.

    Iago.   Nay, but he prated,
And spoke such scurvy and provoking terms
Against your Honor   8
That with the little godliness I have
I did full hard forbear him. But, I pray, sir,
Are you fast married? Be assur'd of this,
That the magnifico is much belov'd,   12
And hath in his effect a voice potential
As double as the duke's. He will divorce you,

---

182 officers of night: *night watchmen*
2 stuff: *substance, essence*   3 contriv'd: *premeditated*
5 yerk'd: *struck (with dagger)*   him; *cf. n.*
12 magnifico: *title of Venetian nobles*   13, 14 *Cf. n.*

Or put upon you what restraint and grievance
The law, with all his might to enforce it on,   16
Will give him cable.

    Oth.   Let him do his spite.
My services which I have done the Signory
Shall out-tongue his complaints. 'Tis yet to know
(Which when I know that boasting is an honor   20
I shall promulgate), I fetch my life and being
From men of royal siege, and my demerits
May speak unbonneted to as proud a fortune
As this that I have reach'd. For know, Iago,   24
But that I love the gentle Desdemona,
I would not my unhoused free condition
Put into circumscription and confine
For the sea's worth. But, look! what lights come yond? 28

    Iago. Those are the raised father and his friends.
You were best go in.

    Oth.   Not I. I must be found.
My parts, my title, and my perfect soul
Shall manifest me rightly. Is it they?   32

    Iago. By Janus, I think no.

    Enter Cassio with lights, Officers and torches.

    Oth. The servants of the duke, and my lieutenant.
The goodness of the night upon you, friends!
What is the news?

---

17 give . . . cable: *permit*   his spite: *whatever spite urges*
18 Signory: *governing body of Venice*
19 'Tis yet to know: *i.e., the world doesn't yet know*
22 siege: *rank*   demerits: *deserts*   23 *Cf. n.*
26 unhoused; *cf. n.*   27 confine: *confinement*
31 parts: *abilities*   perfect: *blameless*
33 Janus: *two-faced Roman god of beginnings*   S.d.; *cf. n.*

Cas.   The duke does greet you, general, 36
And he requires your haste-post-haste appearance,
Even on the instant.
  Oth.   What's the matter, think you?
  Cas. Something from Cyprus, as I may divine.
It is a business of some heat. The galleys   40
Have sent a dozen sequent messengers
This very night at one another's heels,
And many of the consuls, rais'd and met,
Are at the duke's already. You have been hotly call'd for;
When being not at your lodging to be found,   45
The Senate sent above three several quests
To search you out.
  Oth.   'Tis well I'm found by you.
I will but spend a word here in the house,   48
And go with you. [*Enters the Sagittary.*]
  Cas.   Ancient, what makes he here?
  Iago. Faith, he to-night hath boarded a land carrack.
If it prove lawful prize, he's made for ever.
  Cas. I do not understand.
  Iago.   He's married.
  Cas.   To who?   52
  Iago. Marry, to—

[*Re-enter Othello.*]

         Come, captain, will you go?
  Oth.   Have with you.
  Cas. Here comes another troop to seek for you.

40 heat: *urgency*	41 sequent: *successive*
43 consuls: *senators*	
50 carrack: *large merchant vessel*	51 lawful prize; *cf. n.*
52 *Cf. n.*	53 Marry; *cf. n.*

Iago. It is Brabantio. General, be advis'd;
He comes to bad intent.

*Enter Brabantio, Roderigo, and others, with lights and
weapons.*

Oth.   Holla! stand there!   56
Rod. Signior, it is the Moor.
Bra.   Down with him! Thief!
                    [*They draw on both sides.*]
Iago. You, Roderigo! Come, sir, I am for you.
Oth. Keep up your bright swords, for the dew will
    rust 'em.
Good signior, you shall more command with years   60
Than with your weapons.
    Bra. O thou foul thief! Where hast thou stow'd my
    daughter?
Damn'd as thou art, thou hast enchanted her;
For I'll refer me to all things of sense,   64
⟨If she in chains of magic were not bound,⟩
Whether a maid so tender, fair, and happy,
So opposite to marriage that she shunn'd
The wealthy curled darlings of our nation,   68
Would ever have (t'incur a general mock)
Run from her guardage to the sooty bosom
Of such a thing as thou—to fear, not to delight.
⟨Judge me the world, if 'tis not gross in sense   72
That thou hast practis'd on her with foul charms,
Abus'd her delicate youth with drugs or minerals

---

59 Keep up: *keep sheathed*
64 of sense: *capable of judgment*
70 guardage: *guardian's shelter*
72 Judge . . . world: *let the world judge*   gross in sense:
    manifest to the reason

That weaken motion. I'll have't disputed on.
'Tis probable, and palpable to thinking.   76
I therefore apprehend and do attach thee)
For an abuser of the world, a practiser
Of arts inhibited and out of warrant.
Lay hold upon him. If he do resist,   80
Subdue him at his peril.

    Oth.   Hold your hands,
Both you of my inclining and the rest.
Were it my cue to fight, I should have known it
Without a prompter. Wh'er will you that I go   84
To answer this your charge?

    Bra.   To prison, till fit time
Of law and course of direct session
Call thee to answer.

    Oth.   What if I do obey?
How may the duke be therewith satisfied,   88
Whose messengers are here about my side
Upon some present business of the state
To bring me to him?

    Off.   'Tis true, most worthy signior.
The duke's in council, and your noble self,   92
I am sure, is sent for.

    Bra.   How? The duke in council!
In this time of the night! Bring him away.
Mine's not an idle cause. The duke himself,
Or any of my brothers of the state,   96
Cannot but feel this wrong as 'twere their own;

---

75 motion: *inward impulse (cf. I.iii.331)*   have't disputed on:
    refer it to specialists
79 out of warrant: *unwarranted*   84 Wh'er: *whither*
86 course . . . session: *due order of special procedure*

For if such actions may have passage free,
Bondslaves and pagans shall our statesmen be.

Exeunt.

SCENE THIRD

[*The Doge's Palace*]

Enter Duke and Senators, set at a table with lights and Attendants.

Duke. There is no composition in these news
That gives them credit.
   1. Sen.   Indeed, they are disproportion'd.
My letters say a hundred and seven galleys.
   Duke. And mine, a hundred forty.
   2. Sen.   And mine, two hundred.   4
But though they jump not on a just account
(As in these cases, where the aim reports,
'Tis oft with difference), yet do they all confirm
A Turkish fleet, and bearing up to Cyprus.   8
   Duke. Nay, it is possible enough to judgment.
I do not so secure me in the error,
But the main article I do approve
In fearful sense.
   Sailor within. What, ho! what, ho! what, ho!   12
   Off. A messenger from the galleys.

98, 99 *Cf. n.*
Scene Third S.d. Enter . . . Attendants; *cf. n.*
1 composition: *consistency*
5 jump: *agree*   just: *exact*   6 aim: *conjectur*
9 to judgment: *when judicially considered*   10–12 *Cf. n*

Enter Sailor.

Duke.   Now! The business?
Sail. The Turkish preparation makes for Rhodes.
So was I bid report here to the state
⟨By Signior Angelo⟩.   16
   Duke. How say you by this change?
   1. Sen.   This cannot be,
By no assay of reason. 'Tis a pageant
To keep us in false gaze. When we consider
Th'importancy of Cyprus to the Turk,   20
And let ourselves again but understand
That as it more concerns the Turk than Rhodes,
So may he with more facile question bear it,
⟨For that it stands not in such warlike brace,   24
But altogether lacks th'abilities
That Rhodes is dress'd in—if we make thought of this,
We must not think the Turk is so unskilful
To leave that latest which concerns him first,   28
Neglecting an attempt of ease and gain
To wake and wage a danger profitless.⟩
   Duke. Nay, in all confidence, he's not for Rhodes.
   Off. Here is more news.   32

Enter a Messenger.

Mess. The Ottomites, reverend and gracious,
Steering with due course toward the isle of Rhodes,
Have there injointed them with an after fleet⟨.

18 assay of reason: *reasonable test*   pageant: *feigned show*
19 in false gaze: *looking in the wrong direction*
23 with . . . it: *carry it with less effort*
24 brace: *readiness*
30 wake and wage: *start and carry through*   35 after: *reserve*

 1. Sen. Ay, so I thought. How many, as you guess? 36
Mess.) Of thirty sail; and now they do re-stem
Their backward course, bearing with frank appearance
Their purposes toward Cyprus. Signior Montano,
Your trusty and most valiant servitor, 40
With his free duty recommends you thus,
And prays you to believe him.
 Duke. 'Tis certain then, for Cyprus.
Marcus Luccicos is not here in town? 44
 1. Sen. He's now in Florence.
 Duke. Write from us: wish him post-post-haste dis-
  patch.
 1. Sen. Here comes Brabantio and the valiant Moor.

Enter Brabantio, Othello, Cassio, Iago, Roderigo, and
Officers.

 Duke. Valiant Othello, we must straight employ you 48
Against the general enemy Ottoman.
[*To Brabantio.*] I did not see you. Welcome, gentle
  signior;
We lack'd your counsel and your help to-night.
 Bra. So did I yours. Good your Grace, pardon me. 52
Neither my place nor aught I heard of business
Hath rais'd me from my bed, nor doth the general care
Take hold on me, for my particular grief
Is of so floodgate and o'erbearing nature 56
That it engluts and swallows other sorrows
And it is still itself.
 Duke.   Why, what's the matter?
 Bra. My daughter! O my daughter!

41 recommends: *informs*
46 Cf. *n.*   56 floodgate: *torrential*

All.   Dead?

Bra.   Ay, to me.

She is abus'd, stol'n from me, and corrupted   60
By spells and medicines bought of mountebanks;
For nature so preposterously to err
⟨Being not deficient, blind, or lame of sense,⟩
Sans witchcraft could not.   64

   Duke. Whoe'er he be that in this foul proceeding
Hath thus beguil'd your daughter of herself
And you of her, the bloody book of law
You shall yourself read in the bitter letter   68
After your own sense; yea, though our proper son
Stood in your action.

Bra.   Humbly I thank your Grace.
Here is the man, this Moor; whom now, it seems,
Your special mandate for the state affairs   72
Hath hither brought.

All.   We are very sorry for't.

   Duke [to Othello]. What, in your own part, can you
     say to this?

   Bra. Nothing but 'This is so.'

   Oth. Most potent, grave, and reverend signiors,   76
My very noble and approv'd good masters:
That I have ta'en away this old man's daughter,
It is most true; true, I have married her.
The very head and front of my offending   80

61 mountebanks: *itinerant vendors of nostrums; cf. n.*
64 Sans: *without*   could not: *would be impossible*
67–69 Cf. *n.*   69 proper: *own*
70 Stood . . . action: *were involved by your charge*
74 part: *behalf*
76 ff. Cf. *n.*   77 approv'd: *esteemed*
80 head and front: *i.e., the most glaring part*

Hath this extent, no more. Rude am I in my speech,
And little bless'd with the soft phrase of peace,
For since these arms of mine had seven years' pith
Till now some nine moons wasted, they have us'd   84
Their dearest action in the tented field;
And little of this great world can I speak
More than pertains to feats of broil and battle,
And therefore little shall I grace my cause   88
In speaking for myself. Yet, by your gracious patience,
I will a round unvarnish'd tale deliver
Of my whole course of love: what drugs, what charms,
What conjuration, and what mighty magic,   92
(For such proceedings am I charg'd withal)
I won his daughter.

    Bra.   A maiden never bold;
Of spirit so still and quiet, that her motion
Blush'd at herself! And she, in spite of nature,   96
Of years, of country, credit, everything,
To fall in love with what she fear'd to look on!
It is a judgment maim'd and most imperfect
That will confess perfection so could err   100
Against all rules of nature, and must be driven
To find out practices of cunning hell,
Why this should be. I therefore vouch again
That with some mixtures powerful o'er the blood,   104
Or with some dram conjur'd to this effect,
He wrought upon her.

    Duke.   To vouch this is no proof,

---

84 wasted: *past, ago*
91–94 what . . . won: *with what drugs, etc., I won*
93 withal: *with*
95 motion; *cf. n.*   103 vouch: *assert*

Without more certain and more overt test
Than these thin habits and poor likelihoods   108
Of modern seeming do prefer against him.
  1. Sen. But, Othello, speak.
Did you by indirect and forced courses
Subdue and poison this young maid's affections?   112
Or came it by request and such fair question
As soul to soul affordeth?
  Oth.   I do beseech you,
Send for the lady to the Sagittary,
And let her speak of me before her father.   116
If you do find me foul in her report,
⟨The trust, the office I do hold of you,⟩
Not only take away, but let your sentence
Even fall upon my life.
  Duke.   Fetch Desdemona hither.   120
                      Exit two or three.
  Oth. Ancient, conduct them. You best know the place.
                           [Exit Iago.]
And till she come, as truly as to heaven
⟨I do confess the vices of my blood,⟩
So justly to your grave ears I'll present   124
How I did thrive in this fair lady's love,
And she in mine.
  Duke. Say it, Othello.
  Oth. Her father lov'd me; oft invited me,   128
Still question'd me the story of my life

108 thin habits: *insubstantial appearances*
109 modern: *mere, trivial*   111 forced: *violent*
113 question: *conversation*
128 invited me: *entertained me as guest*
129 Still: *constantly*

From year to year, the battles, sieges, fortunes
That I have pass'd.
I ran it through, even from my boyish days   132
To th' very moment that he bade me tell it.
Wherein I spake of most disastrous chances,
Of moving accidents by flood and field,
Of hair-breadth 'scapes i' th' imminent deadly breach, 136
Of being taken by the insolent foe
And sold to slavery, of my redemption thence
And portance in my traveller's history.
Wherein of antres vast and deserts idle,   140
Rough quarries, rocks and hills whose heads touch heaven,
It was my hint to speak (such was the process),
And of the Cannibals that each other eat,
The Anthropophagi, and men whose heads   144
Do grow beneath their shoulders. This to hear
Would Desdemona seriously incline;
But still the house-affairs would draw her thence,
Which ever as she could with haste dispatch   148
She'd come again, and with a greedy ear
Devour up my discourse. Which I observing,
Took once a pliant hour and found good means
To draw from her a prayer of earnest heart   152
That I would all my pilgrimage dilate,
Whereof by parcels she had something heard,
But not intentively. I did consent;
And often did beguile her of her tears,   156

139 portance: *behavior; cf. n.*   140 antres: *caves*
142 hint: *cue*   process: *narrative*
144 Anthropophagi, *etc.; cf. n.*
151 pliant: *suitable*   153 dilate: *relate in full*
154 by parcels: *piecemeal*
155 intentively: *with undistracted attention*

When I did speak of some distressful stroke
That my youth suffer'd. My story being done,
She gave me for my pains a world of sighs.
She swore, i' faith, 'twas strange, 'twas passing strange;
'Twas pitiful, 'twas wondrous pitiful. 161
She wish'd she had not heard it, yet she wish'd
That heaven had made her such a man. She thank'd me,
And bade me, if I had a friend that lov'd her, 164
I should but teach him how to tell my story,
And that would woo her. Upon this heat I spake.
She lov'd me for the dangers I had pass'd,
And I lov'd her that she did pity them. 168
This only is the witchcraft I have us'd.
Here comes the lady; let her witness it.

Enter Desdemona, Iago, and the rest.

Duke. I think this tale would win my daughter too.
Good Brabantio, 172
Take up this mangled matter at the best.
Men do their broken weapons rather use
Than their bare hands.
Bra.   I pray you, hear her speak.
If she confess that she was half the wooer, 176
Destruction on my head, if my bad blame
Light on the man! Come hither, gentle mistress.
Do you perceive in all this noble company
Where most you owe obedience?
Des.   My noble father, 180
I do perceive here a divided duty.
To you I am bound for life and education.

166 Upon this heat: *while the iron was hot; cf. n.*
173 at the best: *as best you may*

My life and education both do learn me
How to respect you: you are the lord of duty,   184
I am hitherto your daughter. But here's my husband;
And so much duty as my mother show'd
To you, preferring you before her father,
So much I challenge that I may profess   188
Due to the Moor my lord.

    Bra.   God be with you! I have done.
Please it your Grace, on to the state affairs.
I had rather to adopt a child than get it.
Come hither, Moor: 192
I here do give thee that with all my heart
⟨Which, but thou hast already, with all my heart⟩
I would keep from thee. For your sake, jewel,
I am glad at soul I have no other child,   196
For thy escape would teach me tyranny,
To hang clogs on 'em. I have done, my lord.

    Duke. Let me speak like yourself and lay a sentence,
Which, as a grise or step, may help these lovers   200
«Into your favor.»
When remedies are past, the griefs are ended
By seeing the worst, which late on hopes depended.
To mourn a mischief that is past and gone   204
Is the next way to draw more mischief on.
What cannot be preserv'd when Fortune takes,
Patience her injury a mockery makes.
The robb'd that smiles steals something from the thief;

---

183 learn: *teach*   191 get: *bege*
197 escape: *escapade*   200 grise: *stai*
202–219 *Cf. n.*   202 griefs: *distresses of mind, anxietie*
203 which: ⟨*refers to 'griefs'*⟩
205 next: *nearest*   more mischief; *cf. n.*
206, 207 *Cf. n.*

He robs himself that spends a bootless grief.   209
   Bra. So let the Turk of Cyprus us beguile,
We lose it not so long as we can smile.
He bears the sentence well that nothing bears   212
But the free comfort which from thence he hears;
But he bears both the sentence and the sorrow
That, to pay grief, must of poor patience borrow.
These sentences, to sugar, or to gall,   216
Being strong on both sides, are equivocal:
But words are words; I never yet did hear
That the bruis'd heart was pierced through the ear.
Beseech you, now to the affairs of state.   220
   Duke. The Turk with a most mighty prepara-
tion makes for Cyprus. Othello, the fortitude of
the place is best known to you; and though we
have there a substitute of most allowed sufficiency,
yet opinion, a sovereign mistress of effects, throws
a more safer voice on you. You must therefore be
content to slubber the gloss of your new fortunes
with this more stubborn and boisterous expedi-
tion.   229
   Oth. The tyrant custom, most grave senators,
Hath made the flinty and steel couch of war
My thrice-driven bed of down. I do agnize   232
A natural and prompt alacrity

209 bootless: *unavailing*   210 let: *i.e., suppose*
212 sentence: *adage (with pun on 'court sentence')*
216, 217 to sugar . . . sides; *cf. n.*
219 pierced: *probed, touched*   220 Cf. n.
225 opinion . . . effects: *reputation, a great producer of results*
227 slubber: *sully*
232 driven: *sifted*   agnize: *acknowledge*
233 alacrity: *congeniality, hearty sympathy*

I find in hardness, and do undertake
These present wars against the Ottomites.
Most humbly therefore bending to your state,   236
I crave fit disposition for my wife,
Due reference of place and exhibition,
With such accommodation and besort
As levels with her breeding.
    Duke.   If you please,   240
Be't at her father's.
    Bra.   I'll not have it so.
    Oth. Nor I.
    Des.   Nor I. I would not there reside,
To put my father in impatient thoughts
By being in his eye. Most gracious duke,   244
To my unfolding lend your prosperous ear,
And let me find a charter in your voice
T'assist my simpleness.
    Duke.   What would you? Speak.
    Des. That I did love the Moor to live with him,   248
My downright violence and storm of fortunes
May trumpet to the world. My heart's subdu'd
Even to the very quality of my lord.
I saw Othello's visage in his mind,   252
And to his honors and his valiant parts
Did I my soul and fortunes consecrate.
So that, dear lords, if I be left behind,
A moth of peace, and he go to the war,   256

234 hardness: *austerity*
238 reference: *assignment*   exhibition: *allowance*
239 besort: *suitable retinue*
245 unfolding: *explanation*   prosperous: *favoring*
246 charter: *official sanction*   249 storm: *forcible seizur*
251 quality: *profession*   256 moth, *etc.; cf. n*

The rites for which I love him are bereft me,
And I a heavy interim shall support
By his dear absence. Let me go with him.

    Oth. Your voices, lords! Beseech you, let her will   260
Have a free way. I therefore beg it not
To please the palate of my appetite,
Nor to comply with heat the young affects
In my distinct and proper satisfaction,   264
But to be free and bounteous to her mind;
And heaven defend your good souls that you think
I will your serious and great business scant
For she is with me. No, when light-wing'd toys   268
Of feather'd Cupid seel with wanton dulness
My speculative and offic'd instruments,
That my disports corrupt and taint my business,
Let housewives make a skillet of my helm,   272
And all indign and base adversities
Make head against my estimation!

    Duke. Be it as you shall privately determine,
Either for her stay or going. Th' affair cries haste,   276
And speed must answer. You must hence to-night.

    «*Des.* To-night, my lord?

    Duke.   This night.»

    Oth.   With all my heart.

---

260 voices: *favorable votes*
263 heat . . . affects: *lust which the young incline to*
264 distinct and proper: *separate and personal; cf. n.*
266 defend: *forbid*
268 For: *because*   toys: *trifles*
269 seel; *cf. n.*
270 speculative . . . instruments: *eyes which should see and perform duties; cf. n.*
272 skillet: *kettle*   helm: *helmet*   273 indign: *unworthy*
274 Make head: *take arms*   estimation: *fame*

Duke. At ten i' the morning here we'll meet again.
Othello, leave some officer behind,   280
And he shall our commission bring to you;
With such things else of quality or respect
As doth concern you.
    Oth.   Please your Grace, my ancient.
A man he is of honesty and trust.   284
To his conveyance I assign my wife,
With what else needful your good Grace shall think
To be sent after me.
    Duke.   Let it be so.
Good night to every one. [*To Brabantio.*] And, noble sig-
        nior,   288
If virtue no delighted beauty lack,
Your son-in-law is far more fair than black.
    1. Sen. Adieu, brave Moor! use Desdemona well.
    Bra. Look to her, Moor, if thou hast eyes to see: 292
She has deceiv'd her father, and may thee.
    Oth. My life upon her faith!
                    Exeunt [*Duke, Senators, Officers, &c.*].
                        Honest Iago,
My Desdemona must I leave to thee:
I prithee, let thy wife attend on her;   296
And bring her after in the best advantage.—
Come, Desdemona; I have but an hour
Of love, of worldly matters and direction
To spend with thee. We must obey the time.   300
                    Ex. Moor and Desdemona.

---

279 ten; *cf. n.*
282 quality or respect: *general importance or detail* (almost
    'genus' *and* 'species')
289 delighted: *delighting*   292, 293 *Cf. n.*

Rod. Iago!

Iago. What sayst thou, noble heart?

Rod. What will I do, think'st thou?

Iago. Why, go to bed, and sleep. 304

Rod. I will incontinently drown myself.

Iago. Well, if thou dost, I shall never love thee after it. Why, thou silly gentleman? 307

Rod. It is silliness to live when to live is a torment; and then have we a prescription to die when death is our physician. 310

Iago. ⟨O, villainous!⟩ I ha' looked upon the world for four times seven years, and since I could distinguish between a benefit and an injury, I never found a man that knew how to love himself. Ere I would say I would drown myself for the love of a guinea-hen, I would change my humanity with a baboon. 317

Rod. What should I do? I confess it is my shame to be so fond, but it is not in my virtue to amend it.

Iago. Virtue! a fig! 'Tis in ourselves that we are thus or thus. Our bodies are gardens, to the which our wills are gardeners; so that if we will plant nettles or sow lettuce, set hyssop and weed up thyme, supply it with one gender of herbs or distract it with many, either to have it sterile with idleness or manured with industry, why, the power and corrigible authority of this lies in our wills. If the balance of our lives had

305 incontinently: *immediately*
316 change: *exchange*
324 gender: *kind*
325 manured: *cultivated*
326 corrigible authority: *correcting control*
327 balance: *weighing instrument*

not one scale of reason to poise another of sensuality,
the blood and baseness of our natures would conduct
us to most preposterous conclusions. But we have
reason to cool our raging motions, our carnal stings,
our unbitted lusts, whereof I take this that you call
love to be a sect or scion.

Rod. It cannot be.   334

Iago. It is merely a lust of the blood and a permission of the will. Come, be a man. Drown thyself?
Drown cats and blind puppies. I profess me thy
friend, and I confess me knit to thy deserving with
cables of perdúrable toughness. I could never better
stead thee than now. Put money in thy purse. Follow
these wars; defeat thy favor with an usurped beard.
I say, put money in thy purse. It cannot be that
Desdemona should long continue her love unto the
Moor,—put money in thy purse,—nor he his to her.
It was a violent commencement, and thou shalt see
an answerable sequestration. Put but money in thy
purse. These Moors are changeable in their wills.
Fill thy purse with money. The food that to him now
is as luscious as locusts, shall be to him shortly as
acerb as the coloquintida. ⟨She must change for
youth.⟩ When she is sated with his body, she will

328 poise: *offset, counterbalance*
331 motions: *impulses*
332 unbitted: *unbridled*
333 sect: *variety*   scion: *off-shoot*
339 perdúrable: *most durable*   340 stead: *aid*
341 defeat thy favor: *disguise thy face*   usurped: *false*
346 answerable sequestration: *similarly hasty parting*
349 locusts: *cassia fistula, a sweet fruit*
350 acerb: *bitter*   coloquintida: *an intensely bitter drug (im-
ported from Cyprus)*

find the error of her choice. «She must have change, she must.» Therefore put money in thy purse. If thou wilt needs damn thyself, do it a more delicate way than drowning. Make all the money thou canst. If sanctimony and a frail vow betwixt an erring barbarian and a supersubtle Venetian be not too hard for my wits and all the tribe of hell, thou shalt enjoy her: therefore make money. A pox o' drowning! 'tis clean out of the way. Seek thou rather to be hanged in compassing thy joy than to be drowned and go without her.   362

Rod. Wilt thou be fast to my hopes ⟨if I depend on the issue⟩?

Iago. Thou art sure of me. Go, make money. I have told thee often, and I tell thee again and again, I hate the Moor. My cause is hearted: thine hath no less reason. Let us be conjunctive in our revenge against him. If thou canst cuckold him, thou dost thyself a pleasure, me a sport. There are many events in the womb of time which will be delivered. Traverse! go! provide thy money! We will have more of this to-morrow. Adieu.   373

Rod. Where shall we meet i' th' morning?

Iago. At my lodging.

Rod. I'll be with thee betimes.   376

Iago. Go to; farewell. Do you hear, Roderigo?

«*Rod.* What say you?

Iago. No more of drowning, do you hear?

---

356 erring: *roving; cf. n. on I.i.136*
367 hearted: *deep-seated in the heart*
368 conjunctive: *united*   369 cuckold him: *seduce his wife*
371 Traverse: *march*   377 Go to: *come, come!*

Rod. I am chang'd.» ⟨I'll sell all my land.⟩   380
   Iago. «Go to; farewell. Put money enough in your
     purse.»   *Exit Roderigo.*
Thus do I ever make my fool my purse;
For I mine own gain'd knowledge should profane,
If I would time expend with such a snipe   384
But for my sport and profit. I hate the Moor,
And it is thought abroad that 'twixt my sheets
He's done my office. I know not if't be true,
But I, for mere suspicion in that kind,   388
Will do as if for surety. He holds me well.
The better shall my purpose work on him.
Cassio's a proper man. Let me see now.—
To get his place, and to plume up my will   392
In double knavery: how? how? Let's see.—
After some time t'abuse Othello's ear
That he is too familiar with his wife.
He has a person and a smooth dispose   396
To be suspected, fram'd to make women false;
The Moor a free and open nature too,
That thinks men honest that but seem to be so,
And will as tenderly be led by th' nose   400
As asses are.
I have't! it is engender'd! Hell and night
Must bring this monstrous birth to the world's light.
                           Exit.

386–389 it is . . . surety; *cf. n.*
388 in that kind: *of that sort*
391 proper: *fine, good-looking*   393 double knavery; *cf. n.*
394 abuse: *deceive*   396 dispose: *manner*

ACT SECOND

SCENE FIRST

*[Famagosta, capital of Cyprus. An open place near
the quay]*

*Enter Montano, Governor of Cyprus, with two other
Gentlemen.*

Mon. What from the cape can you discern at sea?

1. Gent. Nothing at all. It is a high-wrought flood;
I cannot 'twixt the haven and the main
Descry a sail.   4

Mon. Methinks the wind does speak aloud at land;
A fuller blast ne'er shook our battlements.
If it hath ruffian'd so upon the sea,
What ribs of oak, when mountains melt on them,   8
Can hold the mortise? What shall we hear of this?

2. Gent. A segregation of the Turkish fleet;
For do but stand upon the foaming shore,
The chidden billow seems to pelt the clouds;   12
The wind-shak'd surge, with high and monstrous mane,
Seems to cast water on the burning bear
And quench the guards of th' ever-fixed pole.
I never did like molestation view   16

Scene First S.d.; *cf. n.*   3 main: *open ocean; cf. n.*
9 hold the mortise: *remain unshattered*
10 segregation: *dispersal*
15 guards: *two stars in Ursa Minor*   pole: *pole-sta*
16 molestation: *disturbance*

On the enchafed flood.

   Mon.   If that the Turkish fleet
Be not enshelter'd and embay'd, they are drown'd.
It is impossible they bear it out.

Enter a third Gentleman.

   3. Gent. News, lads! our wars are done.   20
The desperate tempest hath so bang'd the Turks
That their designment halts. A noble ship of Venice
Hath seen a grievous wrack and sufferance
On most part of their fleet.   24
   Mon. How! is this true?
   3. Gent.   The ship is here put in,
La Veronesa. Michael Cassio,
Lieutenant to the warlike Moor Othello,
Is come on shore; the Moor himself at sea,   28
And is in full commission here for Cyprus.
   Mon. I am glad on't; 'tis a worthy governor.
   3. Gent. But this same Cassio, though he speak of comfort
Touching the Turkish loss, yet he looks sadly   32
And prays the Moor be safe, for they were parted
With foul and violent tempest.
   Mon.   Pray heaven he be;
For I have serv'd him, and the man commands
Like a full soldier. Let's to the seaside, ho!   36
As well to see the vessel that's come in
As to throw out our eyes for brave Othello,

19 bear it out: *ride it out*
22 designment: *enterprise*   23 sufferance: *disaster*
26 La Veronesa: *'The Lady of Verona' (the ship's name); cf. n.*
36 full: *thorough*

⟨Even till we make the main and th' aerial blue
An indistinct regard.⟩

    3. *Gent.*   Come, let's do so;   40
For every minute is expectancy
Of more arrivance.

Enter Cassio.

   Cas. Thanks to the valiant of this warlike isle,
That so approve the Moor! And let the heavens   44
Give him defence against the elements,
For I have lost him on a dangerous sea.
   Mon. Is he well shipp'd?
   Cas. His bark is stoutly timber'd, and his pilot   48
Of very expert and approv'd allowance.
Therefore my hopes, not surfeited to death,
Stand in bold cure.
   Messenger within. A sail!—a sail!—a sail!

Enter a Messenger.

   Cas. What noise?   52
   Mess. The town is empty. On the brow o' th' sea
Stand ranks of people, and they cry, 'A sail!'
   Cas. My hopes do shape him for the governor.

A shot.

   2. *Gent.* They do discharge the shot of courtesy.   56
Our friends, at least.
   Cas.   I pray you, sir, go forth,
And give us truth who 'tis that is arriv'd.

39, 40 *till the sea and sky become indistinguishable*
42 more arrivance: *further arrivals*
49 *Of very allowed and approved expertness*
50, 51 *Cf. n.*   51 *Messenger; cf. n.*

   2. Gent. I shall.   *Exit.*

   Mon. But, good lieutenant, is your general wiv'd?   60

   Cas. Most fortunately. He hath achiev'd a maid

That paragons description and wild fame;

One that excels the quirks of blazoning pens,

And in th' essential vesture of creation   64

Does tire the ingen-giver.

Enter 2. Gentleman.

                        Now, who has put in?

   2. Gent. 'Tis one Iago, ancient to the general.

   Cas. He's had most favorable and happy speed.

Tempests themselves, high seas, and howling winds,   68

The gutter'd rocks, and congregated sands,

Traitors ensteep'd to clog the guiltless keel,

As having sense of beauty, do omit

Their mortal natures, letting go safely by   72

The divine Desdemona.

   Mon.   What is she?

   Cas. She that I spoke of, our great captain's captain,

Left in the conduct of the bold Iago,

Whose footing here anticipates our thoughts   76

A sennight's speed. Great Jove, Othello guard,

And swell his sail with thine own powerful breath,

That he may bless this bay with his tall ship,

Make love's quick pants in Desdemona's arms,   80

62 paragons: *surpasses*
63 quirks: *subtleties*   blazoning: *extolling*
64 *in the beauties of soul with which nature has clothed her*
65 ingen-giver; *cf. n.*
69 gutter'd: *jagged*
70 ensteep'd: *submerged*   72 mortal: *deadly*
75 conduct: *escort*   77 sennight's: *week's*

Give renew'd fire to our extincted spirits,
«And bring all Cyprus comfort»!

Enter Desdemona, Iago, Emilia, and Roderigo [with Attendants].

                      O! behold,
The riches of the ship is come ashore.
Ye men of Cyprus, let her have your knees.   84
Hail to thee, lady! and the grace of heaven,
Before, behind thee, and on every hand,
Enwheel thee round!
  Des.   I thank you, valiant **Cassio.**
What tidings can you tell me of my lord?   88
  Cas. He is not yet arriv'd; nor know I aught
But that he's well, and will be shortly here.
  Des. O, but I fear! How lost you company?
                  [Cry] within. 'A sail!—a sail!'
  Cas. The great contention of the sea and skies 92
Parted our fellowship. But hark! a sail.   *[Guns heard.]*
  2. Gent. They give their greeting to the citadel:
This likewise is a friend.
  Cas.   «So speaks this voice.» ⟨See for the news!⟩
                        [Exit 2. Gentleman.]
Good ancient, you are welcome. *[Kisses Emilia.]* Welcome, mistress.   96
Let it not gall your patience, good Iago,
That I extend my manners. 'Tis my breeding
That gives me this bold show of courtesy.
  Iago. Sir, would she give you so much of her lips 100
As of her tongue she oft bestows on me,

---

84 knees: *obeisance*   87 Enwheel: *encircle*
95 So . . . news; *cf. n.*   98 extend: *elaborate*

You'd have enough.

 Des.   Alas, she has no speech.

 Iago. In faith, too much.

I find it still when I have list to sleep.   104

Marry, before your ladyship, I grant,

She puts her tongue a little in her heart,

And chides with thinking.

 Emil. You have little cause to say so.   108

 Iago. Come on, come on! You are pictures out o' doors,

Bells in your parlors, wild cats in your kitchens,

Saints in your injuries, devils being offended,

Players in your housewifery, and housewives in your beds.

 Des. O fie upon thee, slanderer!   113

 Iago. Nay, it is true, or else I am a Turk.

You rise to play and go to bed to work.

 Emil. You shall not write my praise.

 Iago.   No, let me not. 116

 Des. What wouldst thou write of me, if thou shouldst
  praise me?

 Iago. O gentle lady, do not put me to't,

For I am nothing if not critical.

 Des. Come on; assay. There's one gone to the harbor?

 Iago. Ay, madam.   121

 Des. I am not merry, but I do beguile

The thing I am by seeming otherwise.

Come, how wouldst thou praise me?   124

---

104 list: *inclination*
109 pictures: *i.e., paint your faces*   110 Bells: *janglers*
111 Saints . . . injuries: *adopt a saintly air when saying spiteful
  things*
112 housewifery, housewives; *cf. n.*
120 assay: *essay, attempt*
123 The . . . am: *my real feeling*

Iago. I am about it, but indeed my invention comes
from my pate as birdlime does from frieze. It plucks
out brains and all. But my muse labors, and thus she
is deliver'd.   128

> If she be fair and wise.—Fairness and wit:
> The one's for use, the other useth it.

Des. Well prais'd! How if she be black and witty?
Iago.

> If she be black, and thereto have a wit,   132
> She'll find a white that shall her blackness fit.

Des. Worse and worse.
Emil. How if fair and foolish?
Iago.

> She never yet was foolish that was fair,   136
> For even her folly help'd her to an heir.

Des. These are old fond paradoxes to make fools
laugh i' th' alehouse. What miserable praise hast thou
for her that's foul and foolish?   140
Iago.

> There's none so foul and foolish thereunto
> But does foul pranks which fair and wise ones do.

Des. O heavy ignorance that praises the worst best!
But what praise couldst thou bestow on a deserving woman indeed? one that, in the authority of

---

125 invention: *imagination*
126 frieze: *rough woolen cloth*   131 black: *brunette*
133 white: *quibble on 'wight' (cf. line 158)*
137 folly: *lewdness*
138 fond: *foolish*
                                                        140 foul: *ugly*

her merits, did justly put on the vouch of very
malice itself?   147
Iago.

> She that was ever fair and never proud,
> Had tongue at will and yet was never loud;
> Never lack'd gold and yet went never gay,   150
> Fled from her wish and yet said 'Now I may';
> She that being anger'd, her revenge being nigh,
> Bade her wrong stay and her displeasure fly;
> She that in wisdom never was so frail   154
> To change the cod's head for the salmon's tail;
> She that could think and ne'er disclose her mind,
> ⟨See suitors following and not look behind:⟩
> She was a wight, if ever such wights were,—

Des. To do what?   159
Iago.

> To suckle fools and chronicle small beer.

Des. O most lame and impotent conclusion! Do
not learn of him, Emilia, though he be thy husband. How say you, Cassio? Is he not a most profane
and liberal counsellor?   164

Cas. He speaks home, madam. You may relish him
more in the soldier than in the scholar.

Iago [*aside*]. He takes her by the palm. Ay, well
said, whisper! With as little a web as this will I ensnare as great a fly as Cassio. Ay, smile upon her, do! I
will gyve thee in thine own courtship. [*Cassio speaks*

---

146 put on: *clothe herself in*   vouch: *favorable testimony*
149 Had tongue at will: *was good at talking*
155 *As to mistake show for substance* (?); *cf. n.*
160 chronicle, *etc.: keep petty household accounts*
164 liberal: *licentious*   165 home: *to the point*
166 in the: *in the character of*   168 said: *done*
169, 170 I . . . courtship; *cf. n.*
170 gyve: *fetter*   courtship: *courtliness*

to Desdemona in dumbshow.] You say true, 'tis so, indeed. If such tricks as these strip you out of your lieu-
tenantry, it had been better you had not kissed your
three fingers so oft, which now again you are most apt
to play the sir in. Very good! well kissed! an excellent
courtesy! 'tis so, indeed. Yet again your fingers to your
lips? would they were clyster-pipes for your sake!

Trumpets within.

The Moor! I know his trumpet.
   Cas. 'Tis truly so.
   Des. Let's meet him and receive him.   180
   Cas. Lo, where he comes!

Enter Othello and Attendants.

Oth. O my fair warrior!
   Des.   My dear Othello!
   Oth. It gives me wonder great as my content
To see you here before me. O my soul's joy,   184
If after every tempest come such calms,
May the winds blow till they have waken'd death!
And let the laboring bark climb hills of seas
Olympus-high, and duck again as low   188
As hell's from heaven! If it were now to die,
'Twere now to be most happy, for I fear
My soul hath her content so absolute
That not another comfort like to this   192
Succeeds in unknown fate.
   Des.   The heavens forbid

174 apt: *ready*   175 sir: *gallant*
177 clyster-pipes: *tubes for injections*
182 warrior: *(because he finds her among the soldiers)*
183 content: *blissful happiness*

But that our loves and comforts should increase
Even as our days do grow.
   Oth.   Amen to that, sweet powers!
I cannot speak enough of this content.   196
It stops me here. It is too much of joy;
And this, and this, the greatest discords be   *They kiss.*
That e'er our hearts shall make!
   Iago [*aside*]. O! you are well tun'd now,   200
But I'll set down the pegs that make this music,
As honest as I am.
   Oth.   Come, let us to the castle.—
News, friends! Our wars are done. The Turks are
    drown'd.
How does my old acquaintance of this isle?—   204
Honey, you shall be well desir'd in Cyprus;
I have found great love amongst them. O my sweet,
I prattle out of fashion, and I dote
In mine own comforts. I prithee, good Iago,   208
Go to the bay and disembark my coffers.
Bring thou the master to the citadel;
He is a good one, and his worthiness
Does challenge much respect. Come, Desdemona! 212
Once more, well met at Cyprus!
        Ex. Othello and Desdemona [*with all except Iago*
                            and Roderigo].

   Iago [*to Rod.*]. Do thou meet me presently at the
harbor. Come hither. If thou be'st valiant (as they
say base men being in love have then a nobility in

197 here: *in his heart*
201 set . . . pegs: *untune the strings by loosening; cf. n.*
205 well desir'd: *much sought after*
210 master: *ship's captain*

their natures more than is native to them), list me.
The lieutenant to-night watches on the court of
guard. First, I must tell thee this: Desdemona is directly in love with him.   220

Rod. With him? Why, 'tis not possible.

Iago. Lay thy finger thus, and let thy soul be in-
structed. Mark me with what violence she first loved
the Moor but for bragging and telling her fantastical
lies. And will she love him still for prating? Let not
thy discreet heart think it. Her eye must be fed; and
what delight shall she have to look on the devil?
When the blood is made dull with the act of sport,
there should be, again to inflame it, and to give
satiety a fresh appetite, loveliness in favor, sympathy
in years, manners, and beauties; all which the Moor is
defective in. Now, for want of these required con-
veniences, her delicate tenderness will find itself
abused, begin to heave the gorge, disrelish and abhor
the Moor. Very nature will instruct her in it, and
compel her to some second choice. Now, sir, this
granted (as it is a most pregnant and unforced position), who stands so eminently in the degree of this
fortune as Cassio does? A knave very voluble, no
farder conscionable than in putting on the mere
form of civil and humane seeming for the better
compassing of his salt and hidden affections? (Why,

217 list: *hear*
218 court: *post*
222 thus: *on the lips (i.e., be silent)*
234 heave the gorge: *be nauseated*
237 pregnant: *obvious*   239 voluble: *fickle*
240 farder: *further*   conscionable: *conscientious*
242 salt: *lewd*

none; why, none.⟩ A subtle, slippery knave, a finder-
out of occasions, that has an eye can stamp and
counterfeit advantages, though true advantage never
present itself. ⟨A devilish knave!⟩ Besides, the knave
is handsome, young, and hath all those requisites in
him that folly and green minds look after. A pestilent
complete knave! and the woman has found him already.   250

Rod. I cannot believe that in her. She's full of
most bless'd condition.

Iago. Bless'd fig's end! The wine she drinks is made
of grapes. If she had been bless'd, she would never
have loved the Moor. ⟨Bless'd pudding!⟩ Didst thou
not see her paddle with the palm of his hand? ⟨Didst
not mark that?⟩   257

Rod. Yes, ⟨that I did;⟩ but that was but courtesy.

Iago. Lechery, by this hand! an index and obscure
prologue to the history of lust and foul thoughts.
They met so near with their lips that their breaths
embraced together. ⟨Villainous thoughts, Roderigo!⟩
When these mutualities so marshal the way, hard at
hand comes the ⟨master and⟩ main exercise, the incorporate conclusion. ⟨Pish!⟩ But, sir, be you ruled
by me: I have brought you from Venice. Watch you
to-night. For your command, I'll lay't upon you.
Cassio knows you not. I'll not be far from you. Do
you find some occasion to anger Cassio, either by

243 A subtle, slippery knave; *cf. n.*
249 found him: *recognized his qualities*
252 condition: *quality*
263 mutualities: *intimacies*   marshal: *lead*
264 incorporate: *carnal*   267 command: *authorization*

speaking too loud, or tainting his discipline, or from
what other cause you please which the time shall
more favorably minister.   272

Rod. Well.

Iago. Sir, he is rash and very sudden in choler,
and haply «with his truncheon» may strike at you.
Provoke him that he may, for even out of that will I
cause these of Cyprus to mutiny, whose qualification
shall come into no true taste again but by the dis-
planting of Cassio. So shall you have a shorter journey to your desires by the means I shall then have to
prefer them, and the impediment most profitably
removed without the which there were no expecta-
tion of our prosperity.   283

Rod. I will do this, if you can bring it to any opportunity.

Iago. I warrant thee. Meet me by and by at the
citadel. I must fetch his necessaries ashore. Farewell.

Rod. Adieu.   *Exit.*

Iago. That Cassio loves her, I do well believe't;   289
That she loves him, 'tis apt, and of great credit.
The Moor (howbeit that I endure him not)
Is of a constant, noble, loving, nature;   292
And I dare think he'll prove to Desdemona
A most dear husband. Now, I do love her too,—
Not out of absolute lust (though peradventure

270 tainting: *disparaging*
272 minister: *provide*
274 in choler: *when enraged*
277 qualification: *pacification*
278 true taste: *satisfactory state; cf. n.*
281 prefer: *promote*   284 if you can; *cf. n.*
290 apt , , · credit: *natural and very credible*

I stand accountant for as great a sin),   296
But partly led to diet my revenge,
For that I do suspect the lusty Moor
Hath leap'd into my seat; the thought whereof
Doth like a poisonous mineral gnaw my inwards,   300
And nothing can nor shall content my soul
Till I am even'd with him, wife for wife,—
Or failing so, yet that I put the Moor
At least into a jealousy so strong   304
That judgment cannot cure. Which thing to do,
If this poor trash of Venice, whom I thrash
For his quick hunting, stand the putting-on,
I'll have our Michael Cassio on the hip,   308
Abuse him to the Moor in the rank garb
(For I fear Cassio with my night-cap too),
Make the Moor thank me, love me, and reward me
For making him egregiously an ass   312
And practising upon his peace and quiet
Even to madness. 'Tis here, but yet confus'd:
Knavery's plain face is never seen till us'd.   *Exit.*

296 accountant: *accountable*   297 diet: *feed*
300 mineral: *drug*   306, 307 whom . . . hunting; *cf. n.*
307 putting-on: *urging; cf. n.*
309 rank garb: *grossest fashion*
313 practising upon: *using wiles against*
314 to madness: *to the point of driving him mad*

SCENE SECOND

[A Street]

Enter Othello's Herald, with a proclamation.

Her. It is Othello's pleasure, our noble and valiant general, that, upon certain tidings now arrived, importing the mere perdition of the Turkish fleet, every man put himself into triumph; some to dance, some 4 to make bonfires, each man to what sport and revels his addiction leads him; for, besides these beneficial news, it is the celebration of his nuptial. So much was his pleasure should be proclaimed. All offices 8 are open, and there is full liberty ⟨of feasting⟩ from this present hour of five till the bell have tolled eleven. Heaven bless the isle of Cyprus and our noble general Othello!   *Exit.*

[SCENE THIRD

The 'Court of Guard' or Guard-post]

Enter Othello, Desdemona, Cassio, and Attendants.

Oth. Good Michael, look you to the guard to-night.
Let's teach ourselves that honorable stop,

3 mere perdition: *complete destruction*
4 put . . . triumph: *give himself up to celebrating the occasion*
6 addiction: *inclination; cf. n.*
8 offices: *storerooms, kitchens*   10 tolled; *cf. n.*
Scene Third; *cf. n.*   2 stop: *caution (musical figure)*

Not to outsport discretion.

Cas. Iago hath direction what to do;   4
But, notwithstanding, with my personal eye
Will I look to't.

Oth.   Iago is most honest.
Michael, good night. To-morrow with your earliest
Let me have speech with you.

          [*To Desdemona.*] Come, my dear love.   8
The purchase made, the fruits are to ensue;
The profit's yet to come 'twixt me and you.
Good night.

          Ex. Othello and Desdemona [and Attendants].

Enter Iago.

Cas. Welcome, Iago; we must to the watch.   12

Iago. Not this hour, lieutenant; 'tis not yet ten
o'clock. Our general cast us thus early for the love
of his Desdemona,—who let us not therefore blame.
He hath not yet made wanton the night with her,
and she is sport for Jove.   17

Cas. She's a most exquisite lady.

Iago. And, I'll warrant her, full of game.

Cas. Indeed, she is a most fresh and delicate
creature.   21

Iago. What an eye she has! Methinks it sounds a
parley of provocation.

Cas. An inviting eye, and yet methinks right
modest.   25

Iago. And when she speaks, is it not an alarum to
love?

15 who: *whom* (Othello)
23 parley: *trumpet-call*   26 alarum: *summons*

Cas. She is indeed perfection. 28

Iago. Well, happiness to their sheets! Come, lieutenant, I have a stoup of wine, and here without are a brace of Cyprus gallants that would fain have a measure to the health of black Othello. 32

Cas. Not to-night, good Iago. I have very poor and unhappy brains for drinking. I could well wish courtesy would invent some other custom of entertainment.

Iago. O they are our friends. But one cup. I'll drink for you.

Cas. I have drunk but one cup to-night, and that was craftily qualified too, and, behold, what innovation it makes here. I am unfortunate in the infirmity, and dare not task my weakness with any more. 42

Iago. What, man! 'tis a night of revels. The gallants desire it.

Cas. Where are they?

Iago. Here at the door. I pray you, call them in. 46

Cas. I'll do't; but it dislikes me. *Exit.*

Iago. If I can fasten but one cup upon him,
With that which he hath drunk to-night already, 49
He'll be as full of quarrel and offence
As my young mistress' dog. Now, my sick fool Roderigo,
Whom love hath turn'd almost the wrong side out, 52
To Desdemona hath to-night carous'd
Potations pottle-deep; and he's to watch.

29 Well, *etc.; cf. n.*
30 stoup: *large measure (often two quarts)*
40 qualified: *diluted*   innovation: *disturbance*
41 here: *in my head*
47 dislikes me: *is distasteful to me*
54 pottle-deep: *to the bottom of the tankard*

Three lads of Cyprus, noble swelling spirits,
That hold their honors in a wary distance,   56
The very elements of this warlike isle,
Have I to-night fluster'd with flowing cups,
And they watch too. Now, 'mongst this flock of drunk-
    ards,
Am I to put our Cassio in some action   60
That may offend the isle. But here they come.
If consequence do but approve my dream,
My boat sails freely, both with wind and stream.

Enter Cassio, Montano, and Gentlemen [*Boys following
    with wine*].

   Cas. 'Fore God, they have given me a rouse already.
   Mon. Good faith, a little one. Not past a pint, as
I am a soldier.   66
   Iago. Some wine, ho!
[*Sings*]

> And let me the canikin clink, clink;
> And let me the canikin clink.
>   A soldier's a man;   70
>   O man's life's but a span;
> Why then let a soldier drink.

Some wine, boys!
   Cas. 'Fore God, an excellent song.
   Iago. I learned it in England, where indeed they
are most potent in potting. Your Dane, your German,

56 Cf. *n.*
57 elements: *typical representatives*
62 Cf. *n.*   64 rouse: *bumper*
68 canikin: *little can or mug (an affectionate diminutive); cf. n.*
76 potent in potting: *mighty in drinking*

and your swag-bellied Hollander,—drink, ho!—are
nothing to your English.   78

   Cas. Is your Englishman so exquisite in his drinking?   80

   Iago. Why, he drinks you with facility your Dane
dead drunk. He sweats not to overthrow your Almain. He gives your Hollander a vomit ere the next
pottle can be filled.   84

   Cas. To the health of our general!

   Mon. I am for it, lieutenant; and I'll do you justice.

   Iago. O sweet England!   88
[*Sings*]

> King Stephen was and——a worthy peer,
>   His breeches cost him but a crown.
> He held them sixpence all too dear,
>   With that he call'd the tailor lown.   92
> He was a wight of high renown,
>   And thou art but of low degree.
> 'Tis pride that pulls the country down,
>   Then take thine owd cloak about thee.   96

Some wine, ho!

   Cas. 'Fore God, this is a more exquisite song than
the other.

   Iago. Will you hear't again?   100

   Cas. No; for I hold him to be unworthy of his
place that does those things. Well, God's above all;
and there be souls must be saved, and there be souls
must not be saved.   104

   Iago. It's true, good lieutenant.

---

77 swag-bellied: *fat-paunched*   82 Almain: *German*
86 do you justice: *keep pace with you in drinking*
92 lown: *loon, lout*   96 owd: *old*

Cas. For mine own part,—no offence to the general, nor any man of quality,—I hope to be saved.

Iago. And so do I too, lieutenant.   108

Cas. Ay; but, by your leave, not before me. The lieutenant is to be saved before the ancient. Let's have no more of this; let's to our affairs. God forgive us our sins! Gentlemen, let's look to our business. Do not think, gentlemen, I am drunk. This is my ancient; this is my right hand, and this is my left hand. I am not drunk now. I can stand well enough, and I speak well enough.   116

Gent. Excellent well.

Cas. Why, very well, then. You must not think then that I am drunk.   *Exit.*

Mon. To the platform, masters. Come, let's set the watch.   120

Iago. You see this fellow that is gone before.
He is a soldier fit to stand by Cæsar
And give direction; and do but see his vice.
'Tis to his virtue a just equinox,   124
The one as long as th' other. 'Tis pity of him.
I fear the trust Othello puts him in,
On some odd time of his infirmity,
Will shake this island.

Mon.   But is he often thus?   128

Iago. 'Tis evermore the prologue to his sleep:
He'll watch the horologe a double set,
If drink rock not his cradle.

120 platform: *rampart*
124 just equinox: *exact equivalent (virtue and vice are equal in
    him)*
130 *Cf. n.*

Mon.   It were well
The general were put in mind of it.   132
Perhaps he sees it not, or his good nature
Prizes the virtue that appears in Cassio,
And looks not on his evils. Is not this true?

Enter Roderigo.

Iago [*aside to him*]. How now, Roderigo?   136
I pray you, after the lieutenant. Go!   *Exit Roderigo.*
    Mon. And 'tis great pity that the noble Moor
Should hazard such a place as his own second
With one of an ingraft infirmity.   140
It were an honest action to say
So to the Moor.
    Iago.   Not I, for this fair island:
I do love Cassio well, and would do much
                        [*Cry*] 'Help! Help!' *within.*
To cure him of this evil. But hark! what noise?   144

Enter Cassio, driving in Roderigo.

    Cas. Zounds! You rogue, you rascal!
    Mon. What's the matter, lieutenant?
    Cas. A knave teach me my duty! I'll beat the knave
into a twiggen bottle.   148
    Rod. Beat me?
    Cas. Dost thou prate, rogue?   [*Striking Roderigo.*]
    Mon. [*Staying him.*] Nay, good lieutenant. I pray
you, sir, hold your hand.   152
    Cas. Let me go, sir, or I'll knock you o'er the maz-
zard.

140 ingraft: *firmly rooted*
148 twiggen bottle; *cf. n.*   153 mazzard: *head*

Mon. Come, come; you're drunk.   155
    Cas. Drunk!   *They fight.*
    Iago [*aside to Roderigo*]. Away, I say! Go out, and
cry a mutiny.   *Exit Roderigo.*
Nay, good lieutenant! God's will, gentlemen!
Help, ho! Lieutenant! Sir Montano! sir!   160
Help, masters! Here's a goodly watch indeed!
                                          A bell rung.

Who's that that rings the bell? *Diablo*, ho!
The town will rise. God's will! lieutenant, hold!
You will be sham'd for ever.   164

        Enter Othello and Gentlemen with weapons.

    Oth.   What is the matter here?
    Mon. Zounds! I bleed still. I am hurt to the death.
    Oth. Hold, for your lives!
    Iago. Hold, hold lieutenant! Sir Montano! gentlemen!
Have you forgot all sense of place and duty?   168
Hold! the general speaks to you; hold for shame!
    Oth. Why, how now, ho! from whence arises this?
Are we turn'd Turks, and to ourselves do that
Which heaven has forbid the Ottomites?   172
For Christian shame put by this barbarous brawl.
He that stirs next to carve for his own rage
Holds his soul light; he dies upon his motion.
Silence that dreadful bell! it frights the isle   176
From her propriety. What's the matter, masters?
Honest Iago, that looks dead with grieving,
Speak, who began this? On thy love, I charge thee.

162 *Diablo; cf. n.*   168 *Cf. n.*
172 *Cf. n.*   174 carve for: *satisfy*
177 From her propriety: *out of her very being*

Iago. I do not know. Friends all but now, even now,
In quarter and in terms like bride and groom   181
Devesting them for bed; and then, but now
(As if some planet had unwitted men)
Swords out, and tilting one at other's breast,   184
In opposition bloody. I cannot speak
Any beginning to this peevish odds,
And would in action glorious I had lost
These legs that brought me to a part of it!   188
　　Oth. How came it, Michael, you were thus forgot?
　　Cas. I pray you, pardon me; I cannot speak.
　　Oth. Worthy Montano, you were wont be civil.
The gravity and stillness of your youth   192
The world hath noted, and your name is great
In mouths of wisest censure. What's the matter,
That you unlace your reputation thus
And spend your rich opinion for the name   196
Of a night-brawler? give me answer to't.
　　Mon. Worthy Othello, I am hurt to danger.
Your officer, Iago, can inform you
(While I spare speech, which something now offends
　　me)   200
Of all that I do know; nor know I aught
By me that's said or done amiss this night,
Unless self-charity be sometime a vice,
And to defend ourselves it be a sin   204
When violence assails us.
　　Oth.　　　　　　　Now, by heaven,

181 In . . . terms: *on a footing*
186 odds: *quarrel*　　　　　　194 censure: *judgment*
195 unlace: *undo*　　　　　　196 opinion: *good name*
200 something: *somewhat*　　offends: *harms*

My blood begins my safer guides to rule,
And passion, having my best judgment collied,
Assays to lead the way. Zounds! If I stir,   208
Or do but lift this arm, the best of you
Shall sink in my rebuke. Give me to know
How this foul rout began, who set it on;
And he that is approv'd in this offence,   212
Though he had twinn'd with me—both at a birth—
Shall lose me. What! in a town of war,
Yet wild, the people's hearts brimful of fear,
To manage private and domestic quarrels   216
In night, and on the court and guard of safety!
'Tis monstrous. Iago, who began't?
    Mon. If partially affin'd, or leagu'd in office,
Thou dost deliver more or less than truth,   220
Thou art no soldier.
    Iago.   Touch me not so near.
I had rather have this tongue cut from my mouth
Than it should do offence to Michael Cassio;
Yet I persuade myself, to speak the truth   224
Shall nothing wrong him. Thus it is, general.
Montano and myself being in speech,
There comes a fellow crying out for help,
And Cassio following him with determin'd sword   228
To execute upon him. Sir, this gentleman
Steps in to Cassio, and entreats his pause.
Myself the crying fellow did pursue,

207 collied: *blackened (as with coal)*
211 rout: *riot*   212 approv'd: *convicted*
216 manage: *set on foot*   217 on . . . safety; *cf. n.*
219 partially affin'd: *bound by partiality*

Lest by his clamor (as it so fell out)   232
The town might fall in fright. He, swift of foot,
Outran my purpose, and I return'd the rather
For that I heard the clink and fall of swords,
And Cassio high in oath, which till to-night   236
I ne'er might say before. When I came back
(For this was brief), I found them close together,
At blow and thrust, even as again they were
When you yourself did part them.   240
More of this matter can I not report,
But men are men; the best sometimes forget.
Though Cassio did some little wrong to him,
As men in rage strike those that wish them best,   244
Yet surely Cassio I, believe, receiv'd
From him that fled some strange indignity,
Which patience could not pass.
   Oth.   I know, Iago,
Thy honesty and love doth mince this matter,   248
Making it light to Cassio. Cassio, I love thee;
But never more be officer of mine—

Enter Desdemona, with others.

Look, if my gentle love be not rais'd up!—
[*To Cassio.*] I'll make thee an example.   252
   Des.   What's the matter?
   Oth. All's well now, sweeting. Come away to bed.—
Sir, for your hurts, myself will be your surgeon.
Lead him off.   [*Montano is led off.*]
Iago, look with care about the town,   256

234 rather: *sooner*   243 him: *i.e., Montano*

And silence those whom this vile brawl distracted.
Come, Desdemona; 'tis the soldiers' life,
To have their balmy slumbers wak'd with strife.

Ex. Moor, Desdemona, and Attendants.

Iago. What! are you hurt, lieutenant?   260

Cas. Ay, past all surgery.

Iago. Marry, God forbid!

Cas. Reputation, reputation, ⟨reputation! O!⟩ I
have lost my reputation. I have lost the immortal
part «sir,» of myself, and what remains is bestial.
My reputation, ⟨Iago, my reputation!⟩   266

Iago. As I am an honest man, I thought you had
received some bodily wound. There is more sense in
that than in reputation. Reputation is an idle and
most false imposition, oft got without merit, and lost
without deserving. You have lost no reputation at
all, unless you repute yourself such a loser. What,
man! there are ways to recover the general again.
You are but now cast in his mood (a punishment
more in policy than in malice), even so as one would
beat his offenceless dog to affright an imperious lion.
Sue to him again, and he is yours.   277

Cas. I will rather sue to be despised than to deceive
so good a commander with so slight, so drunken, and
so indiscreet an officer. ⟨Drunk! and speak parrot!
and squabble, swagger, swear, and discourse fustian
with one's own shadow!⟩ O thou invisible spirit of
wine! if thou hast no name to be known by, let us
call thee devil!   284

270 imposition: *adjunct*   274 mood: *temporary feeling*
280 speak parrot: *use words irrationally*
281 discourse fustian: *talk nonsense*

Iago. What was he that you followed with your sword? What had he done to you?

Cas. I know not.

Iago. Is't possible?   288

Cas. I remember a mass of things, but nothing distinctly; a quarrel, but nothing wherefore. O God! that men should put an enemy in their mouths to steal away their brains; that we should, with joy, revel, pleasure, and applause, transform ourselves into beasts.

Iago. Why, but you are now well enough. How came you thus recovered?   296

Cas. It hath pleased the devil drunkenness to give place to the devil wrath. One unperfectness shows me another, to make me frankly despise myself.   299

Iago. Come, you are too severe a moraler. As the time, the place, and the condition of this country stands, I could heartily wish this had not so befallen, but since it is as it is, mend it for your own good.   303

Cas. I will ask him for my place again. He shall tell me I am a drunkard. Had I as many mouths as Hydra, such an answer would stop them all. To be now a sensible man, by and by a fool, and presently a beast! ⟨O strange!⟩ Every inordinate cup is unblessed and the ingredience is a devil.   309

Iago. Come, come; good wine is a good familiar creature if it be well used. Exclaim no more against it. And, good lieutenant, I think you think I love you.

Cas. I have well approved it, sir. I drunk!   313

Iago. You or any man living may be drunk at some

300 moraler: *moralizer*
306 Hydra; *cf. n.*   310 familiar: *domestic*

time. I'll tell you what you shall do. Our general's
wife is now the general. I may say so in this respect,
for that he has devoted and given up himself to the
contemplation, mark, and denotement of her parts
and graces. Confess yourself freely to her; importune
her help to put you in your place again. She is of so
free, so kind, so apt, so blessed a disposition, that
she holds it a vice in her goodness not to do more
than she is requested. This broken joint between you
and her husband entreat her to splinter; and my fortunes against any lay worth naming, this crack of
your love shall grow stronger than it was before.   326

Cas. You advise me well.

Iago. I protest, in the sincerity of love and honest
kindness.

Cas. I think it freely; and betimes in the morning
will I beseech the virtuous Desdemona to undertake
for me. I am desperate of my fortunes if they check
me here.   333

Iago. You are in the right. Good night, lieutenant;
I must to the watch.

Cas. Good night, honest Iago!   *Exit Cassio.*

Iago. And what's he, then, that says I play the villain,
When this advice is free I give and honest,
Probal to thinking and indeed the course
To win the Moor again? For 'tis most easy   340
Th' inclining Desdemona to subdue
In any honest suit; she's fram'd as fruitful
As the free elements. And then for her

318 denotement: *observation*
324 splinter: *bind with splints*   325 lay: *wager*
339 Probal: *probable*   342 fruitful: *bountiful*

To win the Moor,—were't to renounce his baptism,   344
All seals and symbols of redeemed sin,
His soul is so enfetter'd to her love,
That she may make, unmake, do what she list,
Even as her appetite shall play the god   348
With his weak function. How am I, then, a villain
To counsel Cassio to this parallel course
Directly to his good? Divinity of hell!
When devils will their blackest sins put on,   352
They do suggest at first with heavenly shows,
As I do now; for while this honest fool
Plies Desdemona to repair his fortunes,
And she for him pleads strongly to the Moor,   356
I'll pour this pestilence into his ear
That she repeals him for her body's lust;
And, by how much she strives to do him good,
She shall undo her credit with the Moor.   360
So will I turn her virtue into pitch,
And out of her own goodness make the net
That shall enmesh them all.

Enter Roderigo.

                     How now, Roderigo?   363
   Rod. I do follow here in the chase, not like a
hound that hunts, but one that fills up the cry. My
money is almost spent; I have been to-night exceed-
ingly well cudgelled; and I think the issue will be, I
shall have so much experience for my pains; and so,

349 function: *character*
350 parallel: *straight; cf. n.*   352 put on: *instigate*
353 suggest: *tempt*   358 repeals: *recalls to favor*
365 cry: *pack of hounds (i.e., I merely go through the motions)*

with no money at all and a little more wit, return
again to Venice.

Iago. How poor are they that have not patience!
What wound did ever heal but by degrees?   372
Thou know'st we work by wit and not by witchcraft,
And wit depends on dilatory time.
Does't not go well? Cassio has beaten thee,
And thou by that small hurt hast cashiered Cassio.   376
Though other things grow fair against the sun,
Yet fruits that blossom first will first be ripe.
Content thyself awhile. By the mass, 'tis morning;
Pleasure and action make the hours seem short.   380
Retire thee; go where thou art billeted.
Away, I say; thou shalt know more hereafter.
Nay, get thee gone.   *Exit Roderigo.*
               Two things are to be done:
My wife must move for Cassio to her mistress—   384
I'll set her on—;
Myself awhile to draw the Moor apart,
And bring him jump when he may Cassio find
Soliciting his wife. Ay, that's the way.   388
Dull not device by coldness and delay.   *Exit.*

387 jump: *precisely*

ACT THIRD

SCENE FIRST

[Before the Citadel]

Enter Cassio with Musicians.

Cas. Masters, play here, I will content your pains.
Something that's brief, and bid 'Good morrow, general.'
      They play, and enter the Clown.

 Clo. Why, masters, ha' your instruments been at
Naples, that they speak i' th' nose thus?   4

 Mus. How, sir? how?

 Clo. Are these, I pray, called wind-instruments?

 Mus. Ay, marry, are they, sir.

 Clo. O! thereby hangs a tail.   8

 Mus. Whereby hangs a tale, sir?

 Clo. Marry, sir, by many a wind-instrument that I
know. But, masters, here's money for you; and the
general so likes your music that he desires you, of
all loves, to make no more noise with it.

 Mus. Well, sir, we will not.   14

 Clo. If you have any music that may not be heard,
to't again; but (as they say) to hear music the general does not greatly care.

 Mus. We ha' none such, sir.   18

---

2 S.d. Clown; *cf. n.*   3, 4 Cf. *n.*
12, 13 of all loves: *for goodness' sake*

Clo. Then put up your pipes in your bag, for I'll away. Go; vanish into air; away!   *Exeunt Musicians.*

Cas. Dost thou hear, my honest friend?   21

Clo. No, I hear not your honest friend; I hear you.

Cas. Prithee, keep up thy quillets. There's a poor piece of gold for thee. If the gentlewoman that attends the general's wife be stirring, tell her there's one Cassio entreats her a little favor of speech. Wilt thou do this?   27

Clo. She is stirring, sir. If she will stir hither, I shall seem to notify unto her.

Cas. «Do, good my friend.   *Exit Clown.*

Enter Iago.

In happy time, Iago.

Iago. You ha' not been a-bed, then?

Cas. Why, no. The day had broke   32
Before we parted. I ha' made bold, Iago,
To send in to your wife. My suit to her
Is that she will to virtuous Desdemona
Procure me some accéss.

Iago.   I'll send her to you presently;   36
And I'll devise a mean to draw the Moor
Out of the way, that your converse and business
May be more free.   39

Cas. I humbly thank you for't.   *Exit Iago.*

I never knew
A Florentine more kind and honest.

23 quillets: *quibbles*
25 stirring: *up and dressed (in the morning)*
30 In happy time: *well met*   36 presently: *immediately*
41 Florentine; *cf. n.*

Enter Emilia.

Emil. Good morrow, good lieutenant. I am sorry
For your displeasure; but all will soon be well.
The general and his wife are talking of it,   44
And she speaks for you stoutly. The Moor replies
That he you hurt is of great fame in Cyprus
And great affinity, and that in wholesome wisdom
He might not but refuse you; but he protests he loves you,
And needs no other suitor but his likings   49
«To take the saf'st occasion by the front»
To bring you in again.
    Cas.   Yet, I beseech you,
If you think fit, or that it may be done,   52
Give me advantage of some brief discourse
With Desdemona alone.
    Emil.   Pray you, come in.
I will bestow you where you shall have time
To speak your bosom freely.
    ⟨*Cas.*   I am much bound to you.⟩
                                 Exeunt.

SCENE SECOND

[*A Room in the Citadel*]

Enter Othello, Iago, and other Gentlemen.

Oth. These letters give, Iago, to the pilot,
And by him do my duties to the state.

43 displeasure: *misfortune*
47 affinity: *family connection*   50 Cf. *n.*
56 bosom: *private thoughts and feelings*   2 state; cf. *n.*

That done, I will be walking on the works;
Repair there to me.
    Iago.   Well, my good lord, I'll do't.   4
    Oth. This fortification, gentlemen, shall we see't?
    Gent. We wait upon your lordship.   *Exeunt.*

SCENE THIRD

[The garden of the Citadel]

Enter Desdemona, Cassio, and Emilia.

    Des. Be thou assur'd, good Cassio, I will do
All my abilities in thy behalf.
    Emil. Good madam, do. I know it grieves my husband,
As if the case were his.   4
    Des. O that's an honest fellow! Do not doubt, Cassio,
But I will have my lord and you again
As friendly as you were.
    Cas.   Bounteous madam,
Whatever shall become of Michael Cassio,   8
He's never anything but your true servant.
    Des. O, sir, I thank you. You do love my lord.
You have known him long; and be you well assur'd
He shall in strangeness stand no farther off   12
Than in a politic distance.
    Cas.   Ay, but, lady,
That policy may either last so long,
Or feed upon such nice and waterish diet,

12 strangeness: *estrangement*
14–16 *Cf. n.*   15 nice: *finical*   waterish: *watered, thin*

Or breed itself so out of circumstances,   16
That, I being absent and my place supplied,
My general will forget my love and service.
    Des. Do not doubt that. Before Emilia here
I give thee warrant of thy place. Assure thee,   20
If I do vow a friendship, I'll perform it
To the last article. My lord shall never rest;
I'll watch him tame, and talk him out of patience;
His bed shall seem a school, his board a shrift;   24
I'll intermingle everything he does
With Cassio's suit. Therefore be merry, Cassio;
For thy solicitor shall rather die
Than give thy cause away.   28

       Enter Othello and Iago [at a distance].

    Emil. Madam, here comes my lord.
    Cas. Madam, I'll take my leave.
    Des. Why, stay, and hear me speak.
    Cas. Madam, not now. I am very ill at ease,   32
Unfit for mine own purposes.
    Des. Well, do your discretion.   *Exit Cassio.*
    Iago. Ha! I like not that.
    Oth.   What dost thou say?
    Iago. Nothing, my lord; or if—I know not what.   36
    Oth. Was not that Cassio parted from my wife?
    Iago. Cassio, my lord? No, sure, I cannot think it,
That he would steal away so guilty-like,
Seeing you coming.
    Oth.   I do believe 'twas he.   40

19 doubt: *fear*
23 watch him tame; *cf. n.*   24 shrift: *confessional*
34 do your discretion: *do what seems to you discreet*

Des. How now, my lord!
I have been talking with a suitor here,
A man that languishes in your displeasure.
    Oth. Who is't you mean?   44
    Des. Why, your lieutenant, Cassio. Good my lord,
If I have any grace or power to move you,
His present reconciliation take;
For if he be not one that truly loves you,   48
That errs in ignorance and not in cunning,
I have no judgment in an honest face.
I prithee call him back.
    Oth.   Went he hence now?
    Des. Yes, faith; so humbled,   52
That he has left part of his griefs with me.
I suffer with him. Good love, call him back.
    Oth. Not now, sweet Desdemon. Some other time.
    Des. But shall't be shortly?
    Oth.   The sooner, sweet, for you.   56
    Des. Shall't be to-night at supper?
    Oth.   No, not to-night.
    Des. To-morrow dinner then?
    Oth.   I shall not dine at home.
I meet the captains at the citadel.
    Des. Why then, to-morrow night, or Tuesday morn; 60
On Tuesday noon, or night; on Wednesday morn.
I prithee name the time, but let it not
Exceed three days. I' faith, he's penitent;
And yet his trespass, in our common reason   64
(Save that they say, the wars must make examples
Out of their best), is not almost a fault

60 to-morrow . . . morn; *cf. n.*
66 not almost: *almost not, scarcely*

T' incur a private check. When shall he come?
Tell me, Othello. I wonder in my soul,   68
What you could ask me that I should deny,
Or stand so mammering on. What? Michael Cassio,
That came a-wooing with you, and so many a time,
When I have spoke of you dispraisingly,   72
Hath ta'en your part; to have so much to do
To bring him in! By 'r Lady, I could do much—
   Oth. Prithee, no more! Let him come when he will.
I will deny thee nothing.
   Des.   Why, this is not a boon.   76
'Tis as I should entreat you wear your gloves,
Or feed on nourishing dishes, or keep you warm,
Or sue to you to do a peculiar profit
To your own person. Nay, when I have a suit   80
Wherein I mean to touch your love indeed,
It shall be full of poise and difficúlty,
And fearful to be granted.
   Oth.   I will deny thee nothing.
Whereon, I do beseech thee, grant me this,   84
To leave me but a little to myself.
   Des. Shall I deny you? No. Farewell, my lord.
   Oth. Farewell, my Desdemona. I'll come to thee
    straight.
   Des. Emilia, come. Be it as your fancies teach you.   88
Whate'er you be, I am obedient.
                   Exeunt Desdemona and Emilia.
   Oth. Excellent wretch! Perdition catch my soul
But I do love thee! and when I love thee not,

70 mammering: *hesitating*
74 in: *into favor*   82 poise: *weight*
90 wretch: *expression of utmost fondness*

Chaos is come again.   92

   Iago. My noble lord,—

      Oth.   What dost thou say, Iago?

   Iago. Did Michael Cassio, when you woo'd my lady,

Know of your love?

   Oth. He did, from first to last. Why dost thou ask?   96

   Iago. But for a satisfaction of my thought.

No further harm.

      Oth.   Why of thy thought, Iago?

   Iago. I did not think he had been acquainted with her.

   Oth. O yes; and went between us very oft.   100

   Iago. Indeed?

   Oth. Indeed? ay, indeed. Discern'st thou aught in that?

Is he not honest?

   Iago.   Honest, my lord?

      Oth.   Honest? ay, honest.

   Iago. My lord, for aught I know.   104

   Oth. What dost thou think?

   Iago.   Think, my lord?

      Oth.   Think, my lord?

By heaven, he echoes me,

As if there were some monster in his thought

Too hideous to be shown.—Thou didst mean something.

I heard thee say but now, thou lik'st not that,   109

When Cassio left my wife. What didst not like?

And when I told thee he was of my counsel

In my whole course of wooing, thou criedst, 'Indeed?' 112

And didst contract and purse thy brow together,

As if thou then hadst shut up in thy brain

Some horrible conceit. If thou dost love me,

92 *Cf. n.*   94 *Cf. n.*
111 of my counsel: *in my confidence*   115 conceit: *idea*

Show me thy thought. 116
  Iago. My lord, you know I love you.
  Oth.   I think thou dost;
And, for I know thou'rt full of love and honesty,
And weigh'st thy words before thou give 'em breath,
Therefore these stops of thine fright me the more; 120
For such things in a false disloyal knave
Are tricks of custom, but in a man that's just
They are close delations, working from the heart
That passion cannot rule.
  Iago.   For Michael Cassio, 124
I dare be sworn I think that he is honest.
  Oth. I think so too.
  Iago.   Men should be what they seem;
Or those that be not, would they might seem none!
  Oth. Certain, men should be what they seem. 128
  Iago. Why then, I think Cassio's an honest man.
  Oth. Nay, yet there's more in this.
I pray thee, speak to me as to thy thinkings,
As thou dost ruminate, and give thy worst of thoughts
The worst of words.
  Iago.   Good my lord, pardon me;
Though I am bound to every act of duty,
I am not bound to that all slaves are free to.
Utter my thoughts? Why, say they are vile and false; 136
As where's that palace whereinto foul things
Sometimes intrude not? who has a breast so pure
But some uncleanly apprehensions

120 stops: *pauses, reticences*
122 tricks of custom: *habitual tricks*
123 close delations: *covert, involuntary accusations*
127 seem none; *cf. n.*   139 But: *but therein*

Keep leets and law-days, and in session sit   140
With meditations lawful?

   Oth. Thou dost conspire against thy friend, Iago,
If thou but think'st him wrong'd, and mak'st his ear
A stranger to thy thoughts.

   Iago.   I do beseech you,   144
Though I perchance am vicious in my guess
(As, I confess, it is my nature's plague
To spy into abuses, and oft my jealousy
Shapes faults that are not)—I entreat you then,   148
From one that so imperfectly conjects,
You'ld take no notice, nor build yourself a trouble
Out of my scattering and unsure observance.
It were not for your quiet nor your good,   152
Nor for my manhood, honesty, or wisdom,
To let you know my thoughts.

   Oth.   «Zounds!» ⟨What dost thou mean?⟩

   Iago. Good name in man, and woman, dear my lord,
Is the immediate jewel of our souls.   156
Who steals my purse steals trash. 'Tis something, nothing;
'Twas mine, 'tis his, and has been slave to thousands;
But he that filches from me my good name
Robs me of that which not enriches him,   160
And makes me poor indeed.

   Oth. By heaven, I'll know thy thought.

   Iago. You cannot, if my heart were in your hand;
Nor shall not, whilst 'tis in my custody.   164

   Oth. Ha!

---

140 leets: *synonymous with 'law-days'* (keep leet: *hold court*)
145 Though: *supposing, granting that*   vicious: *wrong*
149 conjects: *imagines; cf. n.*
151 scattering: *random*   156 our souls; *cf. n.*

Iago.   O beware, my lord, of jealousy!
It is the green-ey'd monster which doth mock
The meat it feeds on. That cuckold lives in bliss
Who, certain of his fate, loves not his wronger;   168
But, O, what damned minutes tells he o'er
Who dotes, yet doubts; suspects, yet strongly loves!
    Oth. O misery!
    Iago. Poor and content is rich, and rich enough,   172
But riches fineless is as poor as winter
To him that ever fears he shall be poor.
Good God, the souls of all my tribe defend
From jealousy.
    Oth.   Why, why is this?   176
Think'st thou I'd make a life of jealousy,
To follow still the changes of the moon
With fresh suspicions? No; to be once in doubt
Is once to be resolv'd. Exchange me for a goat   180
When I shall turn the business of my soul
To such exsufflicate and blown surmises,
Matching thy inference. 'Tis not to make me jealous
To say my wife is fair, feeds well, loves company,   184
Is free of speech, sings, plays, and dances well.
Where virtue is, these are more virtuous.
Nor from mine own weak merits will I draw
The smallest fear or doubt of her revolt;   188
For she had eyes and chose me. No, Iago.
I'll see before I doubt; when I doubt, prove;
And, on the proof, there is no more but this:

166, 167 mock . . . feeds on: *tantalizes its victim*
171 O misery; *cf. n.*   173 fineless: *endless*
180 resolv'd: *freed from uncertainty*
182 exsufflicate: *puffed up, empty; cf. n.*

Away at once with love or jealousy!   192
   Iago. I am glad of this; for now I shall have reason
To show the love and duty that I bear you
With franker spirit. Therefore (as I am bound)
Receive it from me—I speak not yet of proof.   196
Look to your wife. Observe her well with Cassio.
Wear your eye thus, not jealous nor secure.
I would not have your free and noble nature
Out of self-bounty be abus'd. Look to't!   200
I know our country disposition well;
In Venice they do let God see the pranks
They dare not show their husbands. Their best conscience
Is not to leave undone, but keep unknown.   204
   Oth. Dost thou say so?
   Iago. She did deceive her father, marrying you:
And when she seem'd to shake and fear your looks,
She lov'd them most.
   Oth.   And so she did.
   Iago.   Why, go to, then.   208
She that so young could give out such a seeming,
To seel her father's eyes up close as oak,—
He thought 'twas witchcraft—but I am much to blame.
I humbly do beseech you of your pardon   212
For too much loving you.
   Oth.   I am bound to thee for ever.
   Iago. I see, this hath a little dash'd your spirits.
   Oth. Not a jot, not a jot.
   Iago.   I' faith, I fear it has.
I hope you will consider what is spoke   216
Comes from my love. But I do see you're mov'd.

195 as I am bound: *this being my duty*
200 self-bounty: *inherent generosity*   201 country: *native*

I am to pray you not to strain my speech
To grosser issues nor to larger reach
Than to suspicion.   220
 Oth. I will not.
 Iago.   Should you do so, my lord,
My speech should fall into such vile success
As my thoughts aim not at. Cassio's my trusty friend—
My lord, I see you're mov'd.
 Oth.   No, not much mov'd.   224
I do not think but Desdemona's honest.
 Iago. Long live she so! and long live you to think so!
 Oth. And, yet, how nature erring from itself,—
 Iago. Ay, there's the point: as (to be bold with you)
Not to affect many proposed matches   229
Of her own clime, complexion, and degree,
Whereto, we see, in all things nature tends—
Foh! one may smell, in such a will, most rank,   232
Foul disproportion, thoughts unnatural.
But pardon me; I do not in position
Distinctly speak of her, though I may fear
Her will, recoiling to her better judgment,   236
May fall to match you with her country forms
And happily repent.
 Oth.   Farewell, farewell.
If more thou dost perceive, let me know more.
Set on thy wife to observe. Leave me, Iago.   240
 Iago. My lord, I take my leave.   [*Going*.]

222 success: *consequences*   225 honest: *virtuous*
234 position: *formal logical thesis*
236 recoiling: *adjusting itself*
237 fall: *chance* country forms: *the types she has been ac-
  customed to*
238 happily: *perhaps*

Oth. Why did I marry? This honest creature, doubtless,
Sees and knows more, much more, than he unfolds.

Iago [*returning*]. My lord, I would I might entreat
  your honor   244
To scan this thing no further; leave it to time.
Though it be fit that Cassio have his place
(For sure he fills it up with great ability),
Yet if you please to hold him off awhile,   248
You shall by that perceive him and his means.
Note if your lady strain his entertainment
With any strong or vehement importunity;
Much will be seen in that. In the mean time,   252
Let me be thought too busy in my fears,
As worthy cause I have to fear I am,
And hold her free, I do beseech your honor.

Oth. Fear not my government.   256

Iago. I once more take my leave.   *Exit.*

Oth. This fellow's of exceeding honesty,
And knows all qualities, with a learned spirit
Of human dealing. If I do prove her haggard,   260
Though that her jesses were my dear heartstrings,
I'd whistle her off and let her down the wind,
To prey at fortune. Haply, for I am black,
And have not those soft parts of conversation   264

249 means: *the methods he uses*
250 strain his entertainment: *urge his reinstatement*
255 free: *guiltless*
256 government: *self control*
259 qualities: *kinds of people*
259, 260 learned . . . dealing: *mind expert in human inter-
    course*
260–263 *Cf. n.*
264 soft . . . conversation: *effeminate talents in social inter-
    course*

That chamberers have, or for I am declin'd
Into the vale of years (yet that's not much)—
She's gone, I am abus'd, and my relief
Must be to loathe her. O curse of marriage!　　　268
That we can call these delicate creatures ours,
And not their appetites. I had rather be a toad,
And live upon the vapor of a dungeon,
Than keep a corner in the thing I love　　　272
For others' uses. Yet, 'tis the plague of great ones;
Prerogativ'd are they less than the base.
'Tis destiny unshunnable, like death:
Even then this forked plague is fated to us　　　276
When we do quicken.
　　　　　　　　　Look, where she comes!
If she be false, O then heaven mocks itself.
I'll not believe't.

Enter Desdemona and Emilia.

Des.　　　　How now, my dear Othello?
Your dinner and the generous islanders　　　280
By you invited do attend your presence.
　Oth. I am to blame.
　Des.　　　　　Why is your speech so faint?
Are you not well?
　Oth. I have a pain upon my forehead here.　　　284
　Des. Faith, that's with watching; 'twill away again.

265 chamberers: *wanton courtiers*
274 Prerogativ'd: *privileged, protected*
276 forked plague: *cuckold's horns*
277 When . . . quicken: *in prenatal life*
280 generous: *noble, of gentle birth*
285 watching: *lack of sleep*

Let me but bind your head; within this hour
It will be well.

   Oth.   Your napkin is too little.

   [*He puts the handkerchief from him, and it drops.*]

Let it alone. Come, I'll go in with you.   288

   Des. I am very sorry that you are not well.

               Exeunt Othello and **Desdemona**

   Emil. I am glad I have found this napkin.
This was her first remembrance from the Moor.
My wayward husband hath a hundred times   292
Woo'd me to steal it, but she so loves the token
(For he conjur'd her she should ever keep it)
That she reserves it evermore about her
To kiss and talk to. I'll have the work ta'en out,   296
And give't Iago.
What he will do with it heaven knows, not I.
I nothing know, but for his fantasy—

             Enter Iago.

   Iago. How now! what do you here alone?   300
   Emil. Do not you chide. I have a thing for you.
   Iago. A thing for me? It is a common thing—
   Emil. Ha?
   Iago. To have a foolish wife.   304
   Emil. O, is that all? What will you give me now
For that same handkerchief?
   Iago.   What handkerchief?

286 your head; *cf. n.*
287 napkin: *handkerchief*
292 a hundred times; *cf. n.*
296 work ta'en out: *embroidery copied*
306 handkerchief; *cf. n.*

Emil. What handkerchief?
Why, that the Moor first gave to Desdemona;   308
That which so often you did bid me steal.
    Iago. Hast stol'n it from her?
    Emil. No, faith. She let it drop by negligence,
And, to th' advantage, I, being here, took't up.   312
Look, here it is.
    Iago.   A good wench! give it me.
    Emil. What will you do with't, that you have been so
        earnest
To have me filch it?
    Iago.   Why, what's that to you?
                                        [*Snatches it.*]
    Emil. If it be not for some purpose of import,   316
Give me't again. Poor lady, she'll run mad
When she shall lack it.
    Iago. Be not acknown on't. I have use for it.
Go, leave me.   *Exit Emilia.*
I will in Cassio's lodging lose this napkin,   321
And let him find it. Trifles light as air
Are to the jealous confirmations strong
As proofs of holy writ; this may do something.   324
⟨The Moor already changes with my poison.⟩
Dangerous conceits are in their natures poisons,
Which at the first are scarce found to distaste,
But, with a little act upon the blood,   328
Burn like the mines of sulphur. I did say so.
Look, where he comes!

319 Be . . . on't: *admit no knowledge of it*
328 with . . . act: *after brief operation*
329 I did say so: *just as I was saying!*

Enter Othello.

                  Not poppy, nor mandragora,
Nor all the drowsy syrups of the world,
Shall ever medicine thee to that sweet sleep   332
Which thou ow'dst yesterday.
    Oth.   Ha! ha! false to me?
    Iago. Why, how now, general? No more of that.
    Oth. Avaunt! be gone! Thou hast set me on the rack.
I swear 'tis better to be much abus'd   336
Than but to know't a little.
    Iago.   How now, my lord?
    Oth. What sense had I of her stol'n hours of lust?
I saw't not, thought it not, it harm'd not me.
I slept the next night well, was free and merry;   340
I found not Cassio's kisses on her lips.
He that is robb'd, not wanting what is stol'n,
Let him not know't and he's not robb'd at all.
    Iago. I am sorry to hear this.   344
    Oth. I had been happy if the general camp,
Píoners and all, had tasted her sweet body,
So I had nothing known. O, now for ever
Farewell the tranquil mind! farewell content!   348
Farewell the plumed troops and the big wars
That make ambition virtue! O, farewell!
Farewell the neighing steed, and the shrill trump,
The spirit-stirring drum, th' ear-piercing fife,   352
The royal banner, and all quality,
Pride, pomp, and circumstance of glorious war!
And, O ye mortal engines, whose wide throats

330 mandragora: *mandrake, a narcotic*   342 wanting: *missing*
346 Píoners: *miners, military menials*
354 circumstance: *ceremony* 355 engines: *cannon* wide; *cf. n*

Th' immortal Jove's great clamor counterfeit,   356
Farewell! Othello's occupation's gone!
   Iago. Is't possible, my lord?
   Oth. Villain, be sure thou prove my love a whore,
Be sure of it! Give me the ocular proof;   360
Or by the worth of man's eternal soul,
Thou hadst been better have been born a dog
Than answer my wak'd wrath.
   Iago.   Is't come to this?
   Oth. Make me to see't; or, at the least, so prove it   364
That the probation bear no hinge nor loop
To hang a doubt on, or woe upon thy life!
   Iago. My noble lord,—
   Oth. If thou dost slander her and torture me,   368
Never pray more. Abandon all remorse;
On horror's head horrors accumulate;
Do deeds to make heaven weep, all earth amaz'd;
For nothing canst thou to damnation add   372
Greater than that.
   Iago.   O grace! O heaven defend me!
Are you a man? Have you a soul or sense?
God be wi' you! Take mine office. O wretched fool!
That liv'st to make thine honesty a vice.   376
O monstrous world! Take note, take note, O world,
To be direct and honest is not safe.
I thank you for this profit, and from hence
I'll love no friend, sith love breeds such offence.   380
   Oth. Nay, stay. Thou shouldst be honest.

---

356 great clamor: *thunder*
365 probation: *proof*   hinge nor loop: *pivot nor strap*
369 remorse: *compunction*   370 accumulate: *pile up*
379 profit: *profitable lesson*   380 sith: *since*

Iago. I should be wise, for honesty's a fool,
And loses that it works for.
⟨*Oth.*   By the world,
I think my wife be honest and think she is not;   384
I think that thou art just and think thou art not.
I'll have some proof. Her name, that was as fresh
As Dian's visage, is now begrim'd and black
As mine own face. If there be cords or knives,   388
Poison or fire or suffocating streams,
I'll not endure it. Would I were satisfied!

Iago. ⟩I see, sir, you are eaten up with passion.
I do repent me that I put it to you.   392
You would be satisfied?
    Oth.   Would? Nay, I will!
Iago. And may; but how? How satisfied, my lord?
Would you, the supervisor, grossly gape on,
Behold her topp'd?
    Oth.   Death and damnation! O!   396
Iago. It were a tedious difficulty, I think,
To bring them to that prospect. Damn them, then,
If ever mortal eyes do see them bolster
More than their own. What then? how then?   400
What shall I say? Where's satisfaction?
It is impossible you should see this,
Were they as prime as goats, as hot as monkeys,
As salt as wolves in pride, and fools as gross   404
As ignorance made drunk. But yet, I say,
If imputation, and strong circumstances,

386 Her; *cf. n.*
392 put: *confided*   399 bolster: *bed (together)*
403 prime: *ardent*   404 in pride: *in heat*
406 imputation . . . circumstances: *opinion based on strong circumstantial evidence*

Which lead directly to the door of truth,
Will give you satisfaction, you may have't.   408
  Oth. Give me a living reason she's disloyal.
  Iago. I do not like the office;
But sith I am enter'd in this cause so far
(Prick'd to't by foolish honesty and love),   412
I will go on. I lay with Cassio lately;
And, being troubled with a raging tooth,
I could not sleep.
There are a kind of men so loose of soul   416
That in their sleeps will mutter their affairs.
One of this kind is Cassio.
In sleep I heard him say, 'Sweet Desdemona,
Let us be wary, let us hide our loves!'   420
And then, sir, would he gripe and wring my hand,
Cry out 'Sweet creature!' and then kiss me hard,
As if he pluck'd up kisses by the roots
That grew upon my lips; then laid his leg   424
Over my thigh, and sigh'd, and kiss'd; and then
Cried, 'Cursed fate, that gave thee to the Moor!'
  Oth. O monstrous! monstrous!
  Iago.   Nay, this was but his dream.
  Oth. But this denoted a foregone conclusion.   428
  Iago. 'Tis a shrewd doubt, though it be but a dream;
And this may help to thicken other proofs
That do demonstrate thinly.
  Oth.   I'll tear her all to pieces!
  Iago. Nay, but be wise. Yet we see nothing done;   432

409 living: *real, not sham*
428 foregone conclusion: *a previous experience*
429 shrewd doubt: *ground for dire suspicion; cf.* n.
430 thicken: *give substance to*

She may be honest yet. Tell me but this:
Have you not sometimes seen a handkerchief
Spotted with strawberries in your wife's hand?

 Oth. I gave her such a one. 'Twas my first gift. 436

 Iago. I know not that; but such a handkerchief
(I am sure it was your wife's) did I to-day
See Cassio wipe his beard with.

 Oth.   If't be that,—

 Iago. If it be that, or any that was hers, 440
It speaks against her with the other proofs.

 Oth. O that the slave had forty thousand lives!
One is too poor, too weak, for my revenge.
Now do I see 'tis true. Look here, Iago; 444
All my fond love thus do I blow to heaven.

       [*Hisses contemptuously.*]

'Tis gone.
Arise, black vengeance, from thy hollow cell!
Yield up, O love, thy crown and hearted throne 448
To tyrannous hate. Swell, bosom, with thy fraught,
For 'tis of aspics' tongues!

 Iago.   Pray, be content.

 Oth. O blood! Iago, blood! 451

 Iago. Patience, I say. Your mind, perhaps, may change.

 Oth. Never ⟨Iago. Like to the Pontic sea,
Whose icy current and compulsive course
Ne'er feels retiring ebb, but keeps due on
To the Propontic and the Hellespont, 456

435 Spotted: *embroidered*
440 any that; *cf. n.*   **442** the slave: *Cassio*
447 hollow cell: *underground prison*
449 fraught: *freight, burden*
450 aspics': *asps', venomous snakes'* content: *quiet*
453–460 *Cf. n.*

Even so my bloody thoughts, with violent pace,
Shall ne'er look back, ne'er ebb to humble love,
Till that a capable and wide revenge
Swallow them up. *He kneels.*
             Now, by yond marble heaven,⟩
In the due reverence of a sacred vow 461
I here engage my words.
  Iago.   Do not rise yet.   *Kneels.*
Witness, you ever-burning lights above!
You elements that clip us round about! 464
Witness that here Iago doth give up
The execution of his wit, hands, heart,
To wrong'd Othello's service! Let him command,
And to obey shall be in me remorse, 468
What bloody work soever.   *[They rise.]*
  Oth.   I greet thy love,
Not with vain thanks, but with acceptance bounteous,
And will upon the instant put thee to't.
Within these three days let me hear thee say 472
That Cassio's not alive.
  Iago. My friend is dead; 'tis done as you request.
But let her live.
  Oth.   Damn her, lewd minx! O, damn her!
Come, go with me apart. I will withdraw 476
To furnish me with some swift means of death
For the fair devil. Now art thou my lieutenant.
  Iago. I am your own for ever.   *Exeunt.*

459 capable: *comprehensive*   460 marble: *inflexible*
464 clip: *enclose*   466 execution: *exercise*
468 remorse: *conscience*   471 to't: *to the test*

SCENE FOURTH

[Before the Citadel]

Enter Desdemona, Emilia, and the Clown.

Des. Do you know, sirrah, where Lieutenant Cassio lies?

Clo. I dare not say he lies anywhere.

Des. Why, man?   4

Clo. He is a soldier, and for one to say a soldier lies is stabbing.

Des. Go to! Where lodges he?

⟨*Clo.* To tell you where he lodges is to tell you where I lie.   9

Des. Can anything be made of this?⟩

Clo. I know not where he lodges, and for me to devise a lodging, and say he lies here or he lies there, were to lie in mine own throat.   13

Des. Can you inquire him out, and be edified by report?

Clo. I will catechize the world for him; that is, make questions, and by them answer.   17

Des. Seek him. Bid him come hither; tell him I have moved my lord in his behalf, and hope all will be well.   20

Clo. To do this is within the compass of man's wit, and therefore I will attempt the doing it.

Exit Clown.

Des. Where should I lose that handkerchief, Emilia?

14, 15 be edified by report: *make intelligent use of what you hear*

Emil. I know not, madam. 24

Des. Believe me, I had rather have lost my purse
Full of cruzadoes; and but my noble Moor
Is true of mind, and made of no such baseness
As jealous creatures are, it were enough 28
To put him to ill thinking.

Emil. Is he not jealous?

Des. Who, he? I think the sun where he was born
Drew all such humors from him.

Emil. Look where he comes!

Des. I will not leave him now till Cassio 32
Be call'd to him.

Enter Othello.

How is't with you, my lord?

Oth. Well, my good lady. [*Aside.*] O hardness to dis-
semble!—
How do you, Desdemona?

Des. Well, my good lord.

Oth. Give me your hand. This hand is moist, my lady.

Des. It yet has felt no age nor known no sorrow. 37

Oth. This argues fruitfulness and liberal heart:
Hot, hot, and moist. This hand of yours requires
A séquester from liberty, fasting and prayer, 40
Much castigation, exercise devout;
For here's a young and sweating devil here
That commonly rebels. 'Tis a good hand,
A frank one.

Des. You may, indeed, say so, 44
For 'twas that hand that gave away my heart.

26 cruzadoes: *Portuguese gold coins*
40 séquester: *separation*

   Oth. A liberal hand! The hearts of old gave hands,
But our new heraldry is hands not hearts.
   Des. I cannot speak of this. Come now, your promise.
   Oth. What promise, chuck?   49
   Des. I have sent to bid Cassio come speak with you.
   Oth. I have a salt and sorry rheum offends me.
Lend me thy handkerchief.
   Des.   Here, my lord.   52
   Oth. That which I gave you.
   Des.   I have it not about me.
   Oth. Not?
   Des.   No, 'faith, my lord.
   Oth.   That is a fault.
That handkerchief
Did an Egyptian to my mother give.   56
She was a charmer and could almost read
The thoughts of people. She told her, while she kept it,
'Twould make her amiable and subdue my father
Entirely to her love, but if she lost it   60
Or made a gift of it, my father's eye
Should hold her loathly, and his spirits should hunt
After new fancies. She dying gave it me;
And bid me, when my fate would have me wive,   64
To give it her. I did so,—and take heed on't;
Make it a darling like your precious eye.
To lose or give't away were such perdition
As nothing else could match.
   Des.   Is't possible?   68

46, 47 Cf. *n.*
49 chuck: *chick (term of endearment)*
51 sorry rheum: *distressing discharge (of eye or nose); cf. n.*
57 charmer: *witch*

Oth. 'Tis true. There's magic in the web of it.
A sibyl, that had number'd in the world
The sun to course two hundred compasses,
In her prophetic fury sew'd the work.   72
The worms were hallow'd that did breed the silk,
And it was dy'd in mummy which the skilful
Conserv'd of maidens' hearts.

   Des.   I' faith? is't true?

   Oth. Most veritable; therefore look to't well.   76

   Des. Then would to God that I had never seen it!

   Oth. Ha? wherefore?

   Des. Why do you speak so startingly and rash?

   Oth. Is 't lost? is 't gone? Speak! Is 't out o' the way? 80

   Des. Heaven bless us!

   Oth.   Say you?

   Des. It is not lost: but what an if it were?

   Oth. How!

   Des. I say, it is not lost.

   Oth.   Fetch't, let me see't.   84

   Des. Why, so I can, sir, but I will not now.
This is a trick to put me from my suit.
Pray you, let Cassio be receiv'd again.

   Oth. Fetch me that handkerchief. My mind misgives.

   Des. Come, come;   89
You'll never meet a more sufficient man.

   «*Oth.* The handkercher!

   Des.   I pray, talk me of Cassio.»

   Oth. The handkerchief!

---

70 sibyl: *inspired prophetess*
71 course . . . compasses: *make . . . revolutions*
74 mummy: *drug made from embalmed bodies*
76 Most veritable; *cf. n.*
79 startingly and rash: *impetuously and fast*

Des.   A man that all his time   92
Hath founded his good fortunes on your love,
Shar'd dangers with you,—
    Oth. The handkerchief!
    Des.   I' faith, you are to blame.
    Oth. Zounds!   *Exit Othello.*
    Emil. Is not this man jealous?   97
    Des. I ne'er saw this before.
Sure, there's some wonder in this handkerchief.
I am most unhappy in the loss of it.   100
    Emil. 'Tis not a year or two shows us a man.
They are all but stomachs, and we all but food.
They eat us hungerly, and when they are full
They belch us. Look you! Cassio and my husband.   104

Enter Iago and Cassio.

Iago. There is no other way; 'tis she must do't.
And, lo, the happiness! Go and impórtune her.
    Des. How now, good Cassio? what's the news with you?
    Cas. Madam, my former suit. I do beseech you   108
That by your virtuous means I may again
Exist, and be a member of his love
Whom I with all the office of my heart
Entirely honor. I would not be delay'd.   112
If my offence be of such mortal kind
That nor my service past, nor present sorrows,
Nor purpos'd merit in futurity,
Can ransom me into his love again,   116
But to know so must be my benefit.

---

100 *Cf. n.*   102 but . . . but: *merely . . . merely*
106 the happiness: *what luck!*   111 office: *duty*
114 nor . . . nor: *neither . . . nor*   117 But: *merely*

So shall I clothe me in a forc'd content,
And shut myself up in some other course
To fortune's alms.
    Des.   Alas, thrice-gentle Cassio,   120
My advocation is not now in tune.
My lord is not my lord; nor should I know him,
Were he in favor as in humor alter'd.
So help me every spirit sanctified,   124
As I have spoken for you all my best
And stood within the blank of his displeasure
For my free speech. You must awhile be patient.
What I can do I will, and more I will   128
Than for myself I dare. Let that suffice you.
    Iago. Is my lord angry?
    Emil.   He went hence but now,
And certainly in strange unquietness.
    Iago. Can he be angry? I have seen the cannon,   132
When it hath blown his ranks into the air,
And, like the devil, from his very arm
Puff'd his own brother,—and can he be angry?
Something of moment then. I will go meet him;   136
There's matter in't indeed, if he be angry.
    Des. I prithee, do so.   *Exit* [*Iago.*]
                   Something, sure, of state,
Either from Venice, or some unhatch'd practice
Made démonstrable here in Cyprus to him,   140
Hath puddled his clear spirit; and in such cases

119 shut . . . in: *confine myself to*
120 To . . . alms: *in pursuit of fortune's favor*
123 humor: *disposition*
126 blank: *range (literally, target)*
139 unhatch'd practice: *undeveloped plot*
141 puddled: *muddied, disturbed*

Men's natures wrangle with inferior things,
Though great ones are their object. 'Tis even so;
For let our finger ache, and it endues 144
Our other healthful members ev'n to that sense
Of pain. Nay, we must think men are not gods,
Nor of them look for such observancy
As fits the bridal. Beshrew me much, Emilia, 148
I was (unhandsome warrior as I am)
Arraigning his unkindness with my soul;
But now I find I had suborn'd the witness,
And he's indicted falsely. 152

   Emil. Pray heaven it be state-matters, as you think,
And no conception, nor no jealous toy
Concerning you.

   Des. Alas the day! I never gave him cause. 156

   Emil. But jealous souls will not be answer'd so.
They are not ever jealous for the cause,
But jealous for they are jealous. 'Tis a monster
Begot upon itself, born on itself. 160

   Des. Heaven keep that monster from Othello's mind!

   Emil. Lady, amen.

   Des. I will go seek him. Cassio, walk hereabout.
If I do find him fit, I'll move your suit 164
And seek to effect it to my uttermost.

   Cas. I humbly thank your ladyship.

                     Exeunt Desdemona and Emilia.

144 endues: *brings*
147 observancy: *tender devotion*
148 Beshrew: *a mild imprecation*
149 unhandsome . . . am: *i.e., failing in this test to be a 'fair warrior'* (cf. II.i.182)
154 conception: *fancy*   toy: *whim*

Enter Bianca.

Bian. 'Save you, friend Cassio!

Cas.   What make you from home?
How is it with you, my most fair Bianca?   168
I' faith, sweet love, I was coming to your house.

Bian. And I was going to your lodging, Cassio.
What! keep a week away? seven days and nights?
Eight score eight hours? and lovers' absent hours,   172
More tedious than the dial eight score times?
O weary reckoning!

Cas.   Pardon me, Bianca,
I have this while with leaden thoughts been press'd,
But I shall, in a more continuate time,   176
Strike off this score of absence. Sweet Bianca,
                [giving her Desdemona's handkerchief]
Take me this work out.

Bian.   O Cassio! whence came this?
This is some token from a newer friend;
To the felt absence now I feel a cause;   180
Is't come to this? ⟨Well, well.⟩

Cas.   Go to, woman!
Throw your vile guesses in the devil's teeth,
From whence you have them. You are jealous now
That this is from some mistress, some remembrance. 184
No, by my faith, Bianca.

Bian.   Why, whose is it?

Cas. I know not, sweet. I found it in my chamber.

167 'Save: *God save, preserve in health*
171 keep a week away; *cf. n.*
172 Eight score eight: *168 (seven times twenty-four)*
176 continuate: *uninterrupted*

I like the work well. Ere it be demanded
(As like enough it will), I'd have it copied.   188
Take it and do't; and leave me for this time.
   Bian. Leave you? wherefore?
   Cas. I do attend here on the general,
And think it no addition nor my wish   192
To have him see me woman'd.
   ⟨*Bian.*   Why, I pray you?
   Cas. Not that I love you not.⟩
   Bian.   But that you do not love me.
I pray you, bring me on the way a little
And say if I shall see you soon at night.   196
   Cas. 'Tis but a little way that I can bring you,
For I attend here; but I'll see you soon.
   Bian. 'Tis very good. I must be circumstanc'd.

                            Exeunt.

ACT FOURTH

SCENE FIRST

[Before the Citadel]

Enter Othello and Iago.

   Iago. Will you think so?
   Oth.   Think so, Iago!
   Iago.   What!

192 no . . . wish: *neither advantageous nor desirable*
193 woman'd: *accompanied by a woman*
199 be circumstanc'd: *yield to circumstances*

To kiss in private?
   Oth.   An unauthoriz'd kiss.
   Iago. Or to be naked with her friend abed
An hour or more, not meaning any harm?   **4**
   Oth. Naked abed, Iago, and not mean harm?
It is hypocrisy against the devil.
They that mean virtuously, and yet do so,
The devil their virtue tempts, and they tempt heaven. **8**
   Iago. So they do nothing, 'tis a venial slip.
But if I give my wife a handkerchief,—
   Oth. What then?
   Iago. Why, then, 'tis hers, my lord; and, being hers,   **12**
She may, I think, bestow't on any man.
   Oth. She is protectress of her honor too.
May she give that?
   Iago. Her honor is an essence that's not seen.   **16**
They have it very oft that have it not;
But for the handkerchief,—
   Oth. By heaven, I would most gladly have forgot it.
Thou said'st (O it comes o'er my memory   **20**
As doth the raven o'er the infected house,
Boding to all) he had my handkerchief.
   Iago. Ay, what of that?
   Oth.   That's not so good now.
   Iago.   **What**
If I had said I had seen him do you wrong?   **24**
Or heard him say (as knaves be such abroad,
Who having, by their own importunate suit
Or voluntary dotage of some mistress,

6 hypocrisy against: *an attempt to cheat*
17 *Cf. n.*
19 *Cf. n.*

Convinced or supplied them, cannot choose   28
But they must blab)—

 Oth.   Hath he said anything?

 Iago. He hath, my lord; but be you well assur'd,
No more than he'll unswear.

 Oth.   What hath he said?

 Iago. Faith, that he did—I know not what he did.   32

 Oth. What? what?

 Iago. Lie—

 Oth. With her?

 Iago.   With her, on her—what you will.

 Oth. Lie with her! lie on her! We say, lie on
her, when they belie her. Lie with her? Zounds,
that's fulsome! Handkerchief!—confessions!—handkerchief! (To confess, and be hanged for his labor.
First, to be hanged, and then to confess: I tremble
at it. Nature would not invest herself in such shad-
owing passion without some instruction. It is not
words that shake me thus. Pish! Noses, ears, and
lips. Is't possible? — Confess! — Handkerchief! — O
devil!)   *Falls in a trance.*

 Iago. Work on,   45
My medicine, work! Thus credulous fools are caught;
And many worthy and chaste dames even thus,
All guiltless, meet reproach. What, ho! my lord!   48
My lord, I say! Othello!

Enter Cassio.

How now, Cassio!

---

28 Convinced: *overcome (those who needed importuning)*
 supplied: *satisfied (those who doted voluntarily)*
35–44 *Cf. n.*

Cas. What's the matter?

Iago. My lord is fallen into an epilepsy.
This is his second fit; he had one yesterday.   52

Cas. Rub him about the temples.

Iago.   «No, forbear.»
The lethargy must have his quiet course.
If not he foams at mouth, and by and by
Breaks out to savage madness. Look! he stirs.   56
Do you withdraw yourself a little while,
He will recover straight. When he is gone,
I would on great occasion speak with you.

                            [*Exit Cassio.*]

How is it, general? Have you not hurt your head?   60

Oth. Dost thou mock me?

Iago.   I mock you! no, by heaven.
Would you would bear your fortunes like a man!

Oth. A horned man's a monster and a beast.

Iago. There's many a beast then, in a populous city, 64
And many a civil monster.

Oth. Did he confess?

Iago.   Good sir, be a man.
Think every bearded fellow that's but yok'd
May draw with you. There's millions now alive   68
That nightly lie in those unproper beds
Which they dare swear peculiar. Your case is better.
O, 'tis the spite of hell, the fiend's arch-mock,
To lip a wanton in a sécure couch,   72

54 his: *its*
63 horned man: *a deceived husband*   65 civil: *civilian*
67 yok'd: *yoked in matrimony*
68 draw: *draw the same cart, endure the same ignominy*
69 unproper: *not their own*
70 peculiar: *their own*   72 lip: *kiss*   sécure: *care-free*

And to suppose her chaste. No, let me know;
And knowing what I am, I know what she shall be.

   Oth. O, thou art wise, 'tis certain.

   Iago.   Stand you awhile apart;
Confine yourself but in a patient list.   76
Whilst you were here o'erwhelmed with your grief
(A passion most unsuiting such a man),
Cassio came hither. I shifted him away,
And laid good 'scuse upon your ecstasy;   80
Bade him anon return and here speak with me,
The which he promis'd. Do but encave yourself,
And mark the fleers, the gibes, and notable scorns
That dwell in every region of his face;   84
For I will make him tell the tale anew,
Where, how, how oft, how long ago, and when
He has, and is again to cope your wife.
I say, but mark his gesture. Marry, patience;   88
Or I shall say you're all in all in spleen,
And nothing of a man.

   Oth.   Dost thou hear, Iago?
I will be found most cunning in my patience,
But—dost thou hear?—most bloody.

   Iago.   That's not amiss;   92
But yet keep time in all. Will you withdraw?

                            [Othello goes apart.]

Now will I question Cassio of Bianca,
A housewife that by selling her desires
Buys herself bread and clothes. It is a creature   96

---

74 what she shall be: *i.e., what I am to call her*
76 patient list: *the bounds of patience*   80 ecstasy: *fit*
82 encave: *conceal*   87 cope: *encounter*
89, 90 all . . . man; *cf. n.*   93 keep time: *proceed fittingly*

That dotes on Cassio (as 'tis the strumpet's plague
To beguile many and be beguil'd by one).
He, when he hears of her, cannot refrain
From the excess of laughter. Here he comes.   100

Enter Cassio.

As he shall smile, Othello shall go mad;
And his unbookish jealousy must cónstrue
Poor Cassio's smiles, gestures, and light behavior
Quite in the wrong. [*Aloud.*] How do you now, lieu-
      tenant?   104
  Cas. The worser that you give me the addition
Whose want even kills me.
  Iago. Ply Desdemona well, and you are sure on't.
[*Speaking lower.*] Now, if this suit lay in Bianca's power,
How quickly should you speed!
  Cas.   Alas! poor caitiff!   109
  Oth. Look how he laughs already!
  Iago. I never knew a woman love man so.
  Cas. Alas! poor rogue! I think, i' faith, she loves me. 112
  Oth. Now he denies it faintly, and laughs it out.
  Iago. Do you hear, Cassio?
  Oth.   Now he impórtunes him
To tell it o'er. Go to! well said, well said.
  Iago. She gives it out that you shall marry her.   116
Do you intend it?
  Cas. Ha, ha, ha!
  Oth. Do you triumph, Roman? do you triumph?   119

102 unbookish: *unskilled*   105 addition: *title*
109 speed: *prosper*   caitiff: *wretch (used pityingly)*
110 *Cf. n.*
119 Roman: *used metaphorically, in association with 'triumph'*

Cas. I marry her! ⟨what? a customer?⟩ I prithee, bear some charity to my wit; do not think it so unwholesome. Ha, ha, ha!

Oth. So, so, so, so. Laugh that wins!

Iago. Faith, the cry goes you shall marry her.   124

Cas. Prithee, say true.

Iago. I am a very villain else.

Oth. Have you scored me? Well!   127

Cas. This is the monkey's own giving out. She is persuaded I will marry her, out of her own love and flattery, not out of my promise.

Oth. Iago beckons me. Now he begins the story.

Cas. She was here even now; she haunts me in every place. I was t'other day talking on the sea bank with certain Venetians, and thither comes the bauble, and falls me thus about my neck—   135

Oth. Crying, 'O dear Cassio!' as it were. His gesture imports it.

Cas. So hangs and lolls and weeps upon me; so hales and pulls me. Ha, ha, ha!   139

Oth. Now he tells how she plucked him to my chamber. O, I see that nose of yours, but not that dog I shall throw it to.

Cas. Well, I must leave her company.

Iago. Before me! look where she comes!   144

Cas. 'Tis such another fitchew! marry, a perfumed one!

120 customer: *prostitute*
121 wit: *intelligence*   unwholesome: *unsound*
123 Laugh: *let him laugh*   127 scored: *notched*
130 flattery: *self-flattery, delusion*   135 bauble: *plaything*
145 such another: *a patronizingly fond intensive, like modern
'such a'*   fitchew: *amorous creature (literally, polecat)*

Enter Bianca.

What do you mean by this haunting of me?   147

Bian. Let the devil and his dam haunt you! What did you mean by that same handkerchief you gave me even now? I was a fine fool to take it. I must take out the work? A likely piece of work, that you should find it in your chamber and not know who left it there! This is some minx's token, and I must take out the work! There, give it your hobby-horse, wheresoever you had it. I'll take out no work on't.

Cas. How now, my sweet Bianca? how now? how now?   157

Oth. By heaven, that should be my handkerchief!

Bian. An you'll come to supper to-night, you may. An you will not, come when you are next prepared for.   *Exit.*

Iago. After her! after her!

Cas. Faith, I must. She'll rail i' the street else.

Iago. Will you sup there?   164

Cas. Faith, I intend so.

Iago. Well, I may chance to see you, for I would very fain speak with you.

Cas. Prithee, come; will you?   168

Iago. Go to! Say no more.   *Exit Cassio.*

Oth. [*advancing*]. How shall I murder him, Iago?

Iago. Did you perceive how he laughed at his vice?

Oth. O Iago!   172

Iago. And did you see the handkerchief?

Oth. Was that mine?

154 hobby-horse: *harlot*
159 An: *if*
160 next: (*implying 'never'*)

⟨*Iago.* Yours, by this hand. And to see how he prizes the foolish woman your wife! She gave it him, and he hath given it his whore.⟩   177

Oth. I would have him nine years a-killing. A fine woman! a fair woman! a sweet woman!

Iago. Nay, you must forget that.   180

Oth. Ay, let her rot and perish, and be damned to-night, for she shall not live. No, my heart is turned to stone. I strike it, and it hurts my hand. O, the world has not a sweeter creature. She might lie by an emperor's side and command him tasks.

Iago. Nay, that's not your way.   186

Oth. Hang her! I do but say what she is. So delicate with her needle! An admirable musician! O, she will sing the savageness out of a bear. Of so high and plenteous wit and invention!   190

Iago. She's the worse for all this.

Oth. O, a thousand, a thousand times. And then, of so gentle a condition!

Iago. Ay, too gentle.   194

Oth. Nay, that's certain. But yet the pity of it, Iago! ⟨O, Iago,⟨ the pity ⟩of it, Iago!⟩

Iago. If you be so fond over her iniquity, give her patent to offend; for, if it touches not you, it comes near nobody.

Oth. I will chop her into messes. Cuckold me—   200

Iago. O, 'tis foul in her.

Oth. With mine officer!

Iago. That's fouler.   203

175–177 Cf. *n.*
186 your way: *the way for you* (*to think of her*)
196 Cf. *n.*   198 patent: *license*

Oth. Get me some poison, Iago, this night. I'll not expostulate with her, lest her body and beauty unprovide my mind again. This night, Iago.

Iago. Do it not with poison. Strangle her in her bed, even the bed she hath contaminated. 208

Oth. Good, good. The justice of it pleases. Very good.

Iago. And for Cassio, let me be his undertaker. You shall hear more by midnight. 212

Oth. Excellent good. *A trumpet.*
                 What trumpet is that same?

Iago. Something from Venice, sure. 'Tis Lodovico, Come from the duke; and see, your wife is with him.

Enter Lodovico, Desdemona, and Attendants.

Lod. God save you, worthy general!
Oth.   With all my heart, sir. 216
Lod. The duke and senators of Venice greet you.
                 [*Gives him a letter.*]
Oth. I kiss the instrument of their pleasures.
              [*Opens the letter and reads.*]
Des. And what's the news, good cousin Lodovico?
Iago. I am very glad to see you, signior. 220
Welcome to Cyprus.
Lod. I thank you. How does Lieutenant Cassio?
Iago. Lives, sir.
Des. Cousin, there's fall'n between him and my lord
An unkind breach, but you shall make all well. 225
Oth. Are you sure of that?
Des. My lord?

205 unprovide: *unfit, weaken*   207 Strangle her; *cf. n.*
211 undertaker: *caretaker (i.e., settle him)*

Oth. [*reads*]. 'This fail you not to do, as you will'— 228

Lod. He did not call. He's busy in the paper.
Is there division 'twixt thy lord and Cassio?

Des. A most unhappy one. I would do much
T'atone them for the love I bear to Cassio.   232

Oth. Fire and brimstone!

Des.   My lord?

Oth.   Are you wise?

Des. What! is he angry?

Lod.   May be the letter mov'd him;
For, as I think, they do command him home,
Deputing Cassio in his government.   236

Des. By my troth, I am glad on't.

Oth.   Indeed?

Des.   My lord?

Oth. I am glad to see you mad.

Des.   How, sweet Othello?

Oth. Devil!   [*Strikes her.*]

Des.   I have not deserved this.

Lod. My lord, this would not be believ'd in Venice, 240
Though I should swear I saw't. 'Tis very much.
Make her amends, she weeps.

Oth.   O devil, devil!
If that the earth could teem with women's tears,
Each drop she falls would prove a crocodile.   244
Out of my sight!

Des. [*going*].   I will not stay to offend you.

228 'This fail you not to do, *etc.; cf. n.*
232 atone: *reconcile*
233 Are you wise: *sardonic; Have you no wisdom?*
236 government: *office*
243 teem with: *be impregnated by*
244 falls: *lets fall*

Lod. Truly, an obedient lady!
I do beseech your lordship, call her back.

   Oth. Mistress!

   Des.   My lord?

   Oth.   What would you with her, sir?

   Lod. Who, I, my lord?   249

   Oth. Ay, you did wish that I would make her turn.
Sir, she can turn, and turn, and yet go on,
And turn again. And she can weep, sir, weep;   252
And she's obedient, as you say, obedient,
Very obedient.—Proceed you in your tears.—
Concerning this, sir,—O well painted passion!—
I am commanded here—Get you away;   256
I'll send for you anon.—Sir, I obey the mandate,
And will return to Venice.—Hence! avaunt!

                        [Exit Desdemona.]
Cassio shall have my place. And, sir, to-night,
I do entreat that we may sup together.   260
You are welcome, sir, to Cyprus.—Goats and monkeys!

                               Exit.

   Lod. Is this the noble Moor whom our full senate
Call all-in-all sufficient? Is this the nature
Whom passion could not shake, whose solid virtue   264
The shot of accident nor dart of chance
Could neither graze nor pierce?

   Iago.   He is much chang'd.

   Lod. Are his wits safe? is he not light of brain?

   Iago. He's that he is. I may not breathe my censure.
What he might be (if what he might he is not)   269
I would to heaven he were!

   Lod.   What! strike his wife!

255 painted passion: *simulated emotion*

Iago. Faith, that was not so well; yet would I knew
That stroke would prove the worst!

Lod.   Is it his use?   272
Or did the letters work upon his blood,
And new-create this fault?

Iago.   Alas, alas!
It is not honesty in me to speak
What I have seen and known. You shall observe him,   276
And his own courses will denote him so
That I may save my speech. Do but go after
And mark how he continues.

Lod. I am sorry that I am deceiv'd in him.   *Exeunt.*

SCENE SECOND

[A Room in the Citadel]

Enter Othello and Emilia.

Oth. You have seen nothing, then?

Emil. Nor ever heard, nor ever did suspect.

Oth. Yes, you have seen Cassio and she together.

Emil. But then I saw no harm, and then I heard   4
Each syllable that breath made up between 'em.

Oth. What! did they never whisper?

Emil.   Never, my lord.

Oth. Nor send you out o' the way?

Emil.   Never.

Oth. To fetch her fan, her gloves, her mask, nor nothing?   8

272 use: *custom*   273 blood: *temper*

Emil. Never, my lord.

Oth. That's strange.

Emil. I durst, my lord, to wager she is honest,
Lay down my soul at stake. If you think other,   12
Remove your thought. It doth abuse your bosom.
If any wretch have put this in your head,
Let heaven requite it with the serpent's curse!
For if she be not honest, chaste, and true,   16
There's no man happy; the purest of their wives
Is foul as slander.

Oth.   Bid her come hither. Go.

                                 Exit Emilia.

She says enough; yet she's a simple bawd
That cannot say as much. This is a subtle whore,   20
A closet lock and key of villainous secrets;
And yet she'll kneel and pray. I have seen her do't.

            Enter Desdemona and Emilia.

Des. My lord, what is your will?

Oth.   Pray, chuck, come hither.

Des. What is your pleasure?

Oth.   Let me see your eyes;   24
Look in my face.

Des.   What horrible fancy's this?

Oth. [*to Emilia*]. Some of your function, mistress.
Leave procreants alone and shut the door;

11 to wager: *in pledge that ('durst' goes with 'Lay down')*
12 other: *otherwise*
15 serpent's curse; *cf. Genesis 3. 14*
20 This: *Emilia*
21 closet lock and key: *instrument of concealment*
26 function: *profession (i.e., of procuress)*

Cough or cry 'hem' if anybody come.   28
Your mystery, your mystery. Nay, dispatch.   *Exit Emilia.*
   Des. Upon my knees, what does your speech import?
I understand a fury in your words
«But not the words».   32
   Oth. Why, what art thou?
   Des.   Your wife, my lord; your true
And loyal wife.
   Oth.   Come, swear it, damn thyself;
Lest, being like one of heaven, the devils themselves
Should fear to seize thee. Therefore be double damn'd.
Swear thou art honest.
   Des.   Heaven doth truly know it.   37
   Oth. Heaven truly knows that thou art false as hell.
   Des. To whom, my lord? with whom? how am I false?
   Oth. Ah! Desdemon! Away, away, away!   40
   Des. Alas, the heavy day! Why do you weep?
Am I the motive of these tears, my lord?
If haply you my father do suspect
An instrument of this your calling back,   44
Lay not your blame on me. If you have lost him,
Why, I have lost him too.
   Oth.   Had it pleas'd heaven
To try me with affliction, had they rain'd
All kinds of sores and shames on my bare head,   48
Steep'd me in poverty to the very lips,
Given to captivity me and my utmost hopes,
I should have found in some part of my soul
A drop of patience. But, alas!, to make me   52

29 mystery: *trade*
42 motive: *cause*   47 they; *cf.* n.
49 Steep'd: *submerged* (*cf.* 'ensteep'd,' II.i.70)

A fixed figure for the time of scorn
To point his slow unmoving fingers at!
Yet could I bear that too. Well! very well!
But there, where I have garner'd up my heart,   56
Where either I must live or bear no life;
The fountain from the which my current runs
Or else dries up: to be discarded thence,
Or keep it as a cistern for foul toads   60
To knot and gender in! Turn thy complexion there,
Patience, thou young and rose-lipp'd cherubin.
I here look grim as hell!
    Des. I hope my noble lord esteems me honest.   64
    Oth. O, ay. As summer flies are in the shambles,
That quicken even with blowing.
O thou black weed, why art so lovely fair?
Thou smell'st so sweet that the sense aches at thee.   68
Would thou hadst ne'er been born!
    Des. Alas, what ignorant sin have I committed?
    Oth. Was this fair paper, this most goodly book,
Made to write 'whore' on? What committed?   72
⟨Committed! O thou public commoner!
I should make very forges of my cheeks,
That would to cinders burn up modesty,
Did I but speak thy deeds. What committed?⟩   76
Heaven stops the nose at it and the moon winks,
The bawdy wind that kisses all it meets
Is hush'd within the hollow mine of earth,

53, 54 Cf. *n.*   56–59 Cf. *n.*
61 gender: *engender, multiply*
61, 62 Turn . . . cherubin; *cf. n.*
62 cherubin; *cf. n.*   63 Cf. *n.*
66 quicken . . . blowing; *cf. n.*
67, 68 O thou black weed . . . sweet; *cf. n.*

And will not hear't. What committed?   80
«Impudent strumpet!»
   Des.   By heaven, you do me wrong.
   Oth. Are not you a strumpet?
   Des.   No, as I am a Christian.
If to preserve this vessel for my lord
From any other foul unlawful touch   84
Be not to be a strumpet, I am none.
   Oth. What! not a whore?
   Des.   No, as I shall be sav'd.
   Oth. Is't possible?
   Des. O heaven, forgiveness!
   Oth.   I cry you mercy, then.   88
I took you for that cunning whore of Venice
That married with Othello. You, mistress,
That have the office opposite to Saint Peter,
And keep the gate of hell!

Enter Emilia.

                   You, you, ay, you!   92
We have done our course. There's money for your pains.
I pray you, turn the key and keep our counsel.   *Exit.*
   Emil. Alas! what does this gentleman conceive?
How do you, madam? how do you, my good lady?   96
   Des. Faith, half asleep.
   Emil. Good madam, what's the matter with my lord?
   Des. With who?
   Emil.   Why, with my lord, madam.

80, 81 What . . . strumpet; *cf. n.*
88 forgiveness: *grant me power to forgive this!*   cry you
   mercy: *ask your pardon* (I cry to be read: Cry)
89 whore of Venice: *a variety with an international fame*
94 turn the key: *open the door*

⟨*Des.* Who is thy lord?

Emil.   He that is yours, sweet lady.

Des. I have none; do not talk to me, Emilia;
I cannot weep, nor answer have I none,
But what should go by water. Prithee, to-night
Lay on my bed our wedding sheets. Remember;   104
And call thy husband hither.

Emil.   Here is a change indeed!

                              Exit.

Des. 'Tis meet I should be us'd so, very meet.
How have I been behav'd, that he might stick
The small'st opinion on my greatest abuse?   108

                Enter Iago and Emilia.

Iago. What is your pleasure, madam? How is't
with you?

Des. I cannot tell. Those that do teach young babes
Do it with gentle means and easy tasks.   112
He might have chid me so, for, in good faith,
I am a child to chiding.

Iago. What is the matter, lady?

Emil. Alas! Iago, my lord hath so bewhor'd her,   116
Thrown such despite and heavy terms upon her,
As true hearts cannot bear.

Des. Am I that name, Iago?

Iago.   What name, fair lady?

Des. Such as she says my lord did say I was.   120

Emil. He call'd her whore. A beggar in his drink

---

103 go by water: *express itself in tears*
107, 108 stick . . . abuse: *even slightly regard my worst of-
    fence as an offence*

Could not have laid such terms upon his callet.

   Iago. Why did he so?

   Des. I do not know. I am sure I am none such.   124

   Iago. Do not weep, do not weep. Alas the day!

   Emil. Has she forsook so many noble matches,
Her father, and her country, and her friends,
To be call'd whore? Would it not make one weep?   128

   Des. It is my wretched fortune.

   Iago.   Beshrew him for't!
How comes this trick upon him?

   Des.   Nay, heaven doth know.

   Emil. I will be hang'd if some eternal villain,
Some busy and insinuating rogue,   132
Some cogging, cozening slave, to get some office
Have not devis'd this slander. I'll be hang'd else.

   Iago. Fie! there is no such man. It is impossible.

   Des. If any such there be, heaven pardon him!   136

   Emil. A halter pardon him, and hell gnaw his bones!
Why should he call her whore? who keeps her company?
What place? what time? what form? what likelihood?
The Moor's abus'd by some outrageous knave,   140
Some base notorious knave, some scurvy fellow.
O heaven! that such companions thou'dst unfold,
And put in every honest hand a whip
To lash the rascal naked through the world,   144
Even from the east to the west!

   Iago.   Speak within doors.

122 callet: *basest of low women*
130 trick: *vagary*
133 cogging, cozening: *deceiving, cheating*   135 *Cf. n.*
141 notorious: *egregious, preëminent*
142 companions: *base fellows*   unfold: *expose*
145 within doors: *quietly, not from the house-tops*

Emil. O, fie upon him! Some such squire he was
That turn'd your wit the seamy side without,
And made you to suspect me with the Moor.   148
 Iago. You are a fool. Go to!
 Des.   O good Iago,
What shall I do to win my lord again?
Good friend, go to him; for, by this light of heaven,
I know not how I lost him. ⟨Here I kneel.   152
If e'er my will did trespass 'gainst his love,
Either in discourse of thought or actual deed,
Or that mine eyes, mine ears, or any sense
Delighted them in any other form;   156
Or that I do not yet, and ever did,
And ever will (though he do shake me off
To beggarly divorcement) love him dearly,
Comfort forswear me! Unkindness may do much;   160
And his unkindness may defeat my life,
But never taint my love. I cannot say 'whore.'
It does abhor me now I speak the word;
To do the act that might th' addition earn   164
Not the world's mass of vanity could make me.⟩
 Iago. I pray you be content. 'Tis but his humor.
The business of the state does him offence
«And he does chide with you».   168
 Des. If 'twere no other,—   [*Trumpets within.*]
 Iago.   'Tis but so, I warr'nt you.
Hark how these instruments summon you to supper,

154 discourse of thought: *day-dreaming*   155 that: *if*
160 Comfort . . . me: *may happiness forsake me*
161 defeat: *destroy*   163 It does abhor me: *I feel abhorrence*
165 vanity: *vain treasure*
168 chide with: *quarrel with, 'take it out on'*

And the great messengers of Venice stay.
Go in, and weep not. All things shall be well.   172

Ex. women.

Enter Roderigo.

How now, Roderigo?

Rod. I do not find that thou deal'st justly with me.

Iago. What in the contrary?   175

Rod. Every day thou daffest me with some device,
Iago; and rather, as it seems to me, thou keepest from
me all conveniency, than suppliest me with the least
advantage of hope. I will indeed no longer endure it,
nor am I yet persuaded to put up in peace what
already I have foolishly suffered.   181

Iago. Will you hear me, Roderigo?

Rod. Faith, I have heard too much, for your words
and performance are no kin together.   184

Iago. You charge me most unjustly.

Rod. ⟨With nought but truth.⟩ I have wasted myself out of my means. The jewels you have had from
me to deliver to Desdemona would half have corrupted a votarist. You have told me she has received
them, and returned me expectations and comforts of
sudden respect and acquittance, but I find none.

Iago. Well, go to! Very well.   192

Rod. Very well? go to? I cannot go to, man; nor

171 stay: *are waiting*
175 *What evidence have you against me?*
176 daffest me: *puttest me off*
178 conveniency: *opportunity*
179 advantage: *increase, furthering*   180 put up: *accept*
182 *Cf. n.*   189 votarist: *religious devotee, nun*
191 sudden respect: *immediate notice*

'tis not very well. By this hand, I say 'tis very scurvy,
and begin to find myself fopped in it.

Iago. Very well. 196

Rod. I tell you 'tis not very well. I will make myself known to Desdemona. If she will return me my
jewels, I will give over my suit and repent my unlawful solicitation. If not, assure yourself I will seek
satisfaction of you. 201

Iago. You have said now?

Rod. Ay, and said nothing but what I protest in-
tendment of doing. 204

Iago. Why, now I see there's mettle in thee, and
even from this instant do build on thee a better
opinion than ever before. Give me thy hand, Roderigo. Thou hast taken against me a most just excep-
tion; but yet, I protest, I have dealt most directly in
thy affair. 210

Rod. It hath not appeared.

Iago. I grant indeed it hath not appeared, and your
suspicion is not without wit and judgment. But,
Roderigo, if thou hast that within thee indeed, which
I have greater reason to believe now than ever (I
mean purpose, courage, and valor), this night show
it. If thou the next night following enjoyest not Desdemona, take me from this world with treachery and
devise engines for my life. 219

Rod. Well, ⟨what is it?⟩ is it within reason and
compass?

Iago. Sir, there is especial commission come from
Venice to depute Cassio in Othello's place. 223

195 fopped: *swindled*   202 said: *finished your speech*
209 directly: *straightforwardly*   219 engines for: *plots against*

Rod. Is that true? Why, then Othello and Desdemona return again to Venice.

Iago. O, no! he goes into Mauritania, and takes
away with him the fair Desdemona, unless his abode
be lingered here by some accident; wherein none can
be so determinate as the removing of Cassio.

Rod. How do you mean, removing of him?   230

Iago. Why, by making him uncapable of Othello's
place. Knocking out his brains.

Rod. And that you would have me to do!   233

Iago. Ay; if you dare do yourself a profit and right.
He sups to-night with a harlotry, and thither will I
go to him. He knows not yet of his honorable fortune.
If you will watch his going thence (which I will
fashion to fall out between twelve and one), you
may take him at your pleasure. I will be near to second your attempt, and he shall fall between us.
Come, stand not amazed at it, but go along with me. I
will show you such a necessity in his death that you
shall think yourself bound to put it on him. It is now
high supper-time, and the night grows to waste.
About it.   245

Rod. I will hear further reason for this.

Iago. And you shall be satisfied.   *Exeunt.*

226 Mauritania: *supposed land of the Moors; cf. n.*
228 lingered: *prolonged*   229 determinate: *decisive*
244 grows to waste: *is wasting away*

SCENE THIRD

[*State Bedroom in the Citadel*]

Enter Othello, Lodovico, Desdemona, Emilia, and Attendants.

Lod. I do beseech you, sir, trouble yourself no further.
Oth. O pardon me; 'twill do me good to walk.
Lod. Madam, good night. I humbly thank your ladyship.
Des. Your honor is most welcome.
Oth.   Will you walk, sir?—
O! Desdemona.   5
Des. My lord?
    Oth. Get you to bed o' the instant. I will be returned forthwith. Dispatch your attendant there.
Look it be done.   9
Des. I will, my lord.
            Exit [*Othello, with Lodovico and Attendants*].
Emil. How goes it now? He looks gentler than he did.
Des. He says he will return incontinent.   12
He hath commanded me to go to bed,
And bade me to dismiss you.
    Emil.   Dismiss me!
Des. It was his bidding. Therefore, good Emilia,
Give me my nightly wearing, and adieu.   16
We must not now displease him.

Cf. n.   2 pardon me: *don't mention it*
Will you walk: *shall we start?*
dispatch: 'dismiss' (Folio)   12 incontinent: *immediately*

Emil. I would you had never seen him.

Des. So would not I. My love doth so approve him,
That even his stubbornness, his checks and frowns,—   20
Prithee, unpin me,—have grace and favor in them.

Emil. I have laid those sheets you bade me on the bed.

Des. All's one. Good faith! how foolish are our minds!
If I do die before thee, prithee, shroud me   24
In one of those same sheets.

Emil.   Come, come, you talk!

Des. My mother had a maid call'd Barbary:
She was in love, and he she lov'd prov'd mad
And did forsake her. She had a song of 'willow';   28
An old thing 'twas, but it express'd her fortune,
And she died singing it. That song to-night
Will not go from my mind. ⟨I have much to do
But to go hang my head all at one side,   32
And sing it like poor Barbary. Prithee, dispatch.

Emil. Shall I go fetch your night-gown?

Des.   No, unpin me here.
This Lodovico is a proper man.

Emil. A very handsome man.   36

Des. He speaks well.

Emil. I know a lady in Venice would have walked
barefoot to Palestine for a touch of his nether lip.

Desdemona sings.

The poor soul sat sighing by a sycamore tree,—   40
  Sing all a green willow.
Her hand on her bosom, her head on her knee,—
  Sing willow, willow, willow.

23 All's one: *no matter*   25 talk: *talk idl*
27 mad: *inconstant, wild*   29 An old thing 'twas; cf. *n*
32 But to: *not to*

The fresh streams ran by her, and murmur'd her moans. 44
   Sing willow, &c.
Her salt tears fell from her, and soften'd the stones.
   Sing willow, &c.

⌐ay by these.—   48

             Willow, willow.

'rithee, hie thee; he'll come anon.

    Sing all a green willow must be my garland.
    Let nobody blame him, his scorn I approve,—   52

Nay, that's not next.) Hark! who is it that knocks?
   Emil. It is the wind.
Des.

   ⟨I call'd my love false love; but what said he then?
     Sing willow, &c.   56
   If I court mo women, you'll couch with mo men.⟩

Now get thee gone. Good night. Mine eyes do itch;
Does that bode weeping?
   Emil.   'Tis neither here nor there.
⟨*Des.* I have heard it said so. O these men, these men!
Dost thou in conscience think (tell me, Emilia)   61
That there be women do abuse their husbands
In such gross kind?
   Emil.   There be some such, no question.⟩
Des. Wouldst thou do such a deed for all the world? 64
Emil. Why, would not you?
Des.   No, by this heavenly light!
   Emil. Nor I neither by this heavenly light. I might
do't as well i' th' dark.   67
Des. Wouldst thou do such a deed for all the world?

⌐ hie thee: *make haste*

Emil. The world is a huge thing. It is a great price
for a small vice.

Des. Good troth, I think thou wouldst not.   71

Emil. By my troth, I think I should, and undo't
when I had done it. Marry, I would not do such a
thing for a joint-ring, nor for measures of lawn, nor
for gowns, petticoats, nor caps, nor any petty exhibition. But for the whole world? Ud's pity! who would
not make her husband a cuckold to make him a
monarch? I should venture purgatory for't.   7

Des. Beshrew me, if I would do such a wrong
For the whole world.

Emil. Why, the wrong is but a wrong i' the world;
and having the world for your labor, 'tis a wrong in
your own world, and you might quickly make it right.

Des. I do not think there is any such woman.   8.

Emil. Yes, a dozen; and as many to the vantage,
as would store the world they played for.

⟨But I do think it is their husbands' faults
If wives do fall. Say that they slack their duties,   8
And pour our treasures into foreign laps,
Or else break out in peevish jealousies,
Throwing restraint upon us; or say they strike us,
Or scant our former having in despite;   9
Why, we have galls, and though we have some grace,
Yet have we some revenge. Let husbands know
Their wives have sense like them. They see and smell,

72, 73 undo't . . . done: *see lines 81–83*
74 joint-ring: *ring made in interlocking halves*
85 to the vantage: *to boot, in addition*
92 having: *allowance, pin-money*   despite: *spite*
93 galls: *spirit to resent injury*
95 sense: *sensations, feelings*

And have their palates both for sweet and sour, 96
As husbands have. What is it that they do
When they change us for others? Is it sport?
I think it is. And doth affection breed it?
I think it doth. Is't frailty that thus errs? 100
It is so too. And have not we affections,
Desires for sport, and frailty as men have?
Then, let them use us well; else let them know,
The ills we do, their ills instruct us so.) 104
   Des. Good night, good night! God me such usage send,
Not to pick bad from bad, but by bad mend!   *Exeunt.*

ACT FIFTH

SCENE FIRST

[*A Street near Bianca's lodging*]

Enter Iago and Roderigo.

   Iago. Here, stand behind this bulk. Straight will he
come.
Wear thy good rapier bare, and put it home.
Quick, quick. Fear nothing; I'll be at thy elbow.
It makes us, or it mars us. Think of that, 4
And fix most firm thy resolution.
   Rod. Be near at hand. I may miscarry in't.
   Iago. Here, at thy hand. Be bold, and take thy stand.
                              [*Retires.*]

99 affection: *inclination*   105 usage: *code of conduct*
106 Cf. *n.*   1 bulk: *projecting shelter*

Rod. I have no great devotion to the deed;   8
And yet he has given me satisfying reasons.
'Tis but a man gone. Forth, my sword! he dies.

Iago. I have rubb'd this young quat almost to the sense,
And he grows angry. Now, whether he kill Cassio,   12
Or Cassio him, or each do kill the other,
Every way makes my gain. Live Roderigo,
He calls me to a restitution large
Of gold and jewels that I bobb'd from him,   16
As gifts to Desdemona.
It must not be. If Cassio do remain,
He has a daily beauty in his life
That makes me ugly; and, besides, the Moor   20
May unfold me to him. There stand I in peril.
No, he must die. Be it so! I hear him coming.

Enter Cassio.

Rod. I know his gait; 'tis he. Villain, thou diest!
                    [*Makes a pass at Cassio.*]

Cas. That thrust had been my enemy indeed   24
But that my coat is better than thou think'st.
I will make proof of thine.
                    [*Draws, and wounds Roderigo.*]
Rod.   O! I am slain!
    [*Iago from behind wounds Cassio in the leg, and exit.*]
Cas. I am maim'd for ever! Light, ho! murder! murder!
                    [*Falls.*]

11 quat: *pimple* (*cf. modern 'scab'*)   sense: *quick*
14 *Cf. n.* Live Roderigo: *if Roderigo live*
16 bobb'd from him: *cheated him out of*
19 *Cf. n.*
25 coat: *i.e., he wore defensive armor under his outer garments*

Enter Othello [at a distance].

Oth. The voice of Cassio. Iago keeps his word.

Rod. O villain that I am!

Oth.   Hark! 'Tis even so.   29

Cas. O, help, ho! light! a surgeon!

Oth. 'Tis he. O brave Iago, honest and just,

That hast such noble sense of thy friend's wrong!   32

Thou teachest me. Minion, your dear lies dead,

And your fate hies apace. Strumpet, I come!

Forth of my heart those charms, thine eyes, are blotted.

Thy bed, lust-stain'd, shall with lust's blood be spotted. 36

                                        Exit Othello.

Enter Lodovico and Gratiano [at a distance].

Cas. What ho! no watch? no passage? murder! murder!

Gra. 'Tis some mischance. The cry is very direful.

Cas. O, help!

Lod. Hark!   40

Rod. O wretched villain!

Lod. Two or three groan. It is a heavy night;

These may be counterfeits. Let's think't unsafe

To come in to the cry without more help.   44

Rod. Nobody come? then shall I bleed to death.

Lod. Hark!

Enter Iago, with a light.

Gra. Here's one comes in his shirt, with light and
weapons.

Iago. Who's there? Whose noise is this that cries on
murder?   48

27 S.d. Enter Othello; *cf. n.*
33 Minion: *hussy*   37 passage: *passers-by*
42 heavy: *doleful (cf. V.ii.98)*   48 cries on: *shouts*

Lod. We do not know.

Iago.   Did not you hear a cry?

Cas. Here, here! For heaven's sake, help me.

Iago.   What's the matter?

Gra. This is Othello's ancient, as I take it.

Lod. The same indeed. A very valiant fellow.

Iago. What are you here that cry so grievously?   53

Cas. Iago? O, I am spoil'd, undone by villains!
Give me some help.

Iago. O my lieutenant! what villains have done this?   56

Cas. I think that one of them is hereabout,
And cannot make away.

Iago.   O treacherous villains!
[*To Lodovico and Gratiano.*] What are you there? Come
   in, and give some help.

Rod. O help me here!   60

Cas. That's one of them.

Iago.   O murderous slave! O villain!
                                   [*Stabs Roderigo.*]

Rod. O damn'd Iago! O inhuman dog!

Iago. Kill men i' the dark! Where be those bloody
   thieves?
How silent is this town! Ho! murder! murder!
What may you be? are you of good or evil?   65

Lod. As you shall prove us, praise us.

Iago. Signior Lodovico?

Lod. He, sir.   68

Iago. I cry you mercy. Here's Cassio hurt by villains.

Gra. Cassio?

Iago. How is it, brother?

59 What: *who*
66 praise: *appraise, estimate*

Cas. My leg is cut in two.

Iago.   Marry, heaven forbid!   72
Light, gentlemen. I'll bind it with my shirt.

Enter Bianca.

Bian. What is the matter, ho? who is't that cried?

Iago. Who is't that cried!

Bian. O my dear Cassio! O my sweet Cassio!   76
Cassio! Cassio!

Iago. O notable strumpet! Cassio, may you suspect
Who they should be that thus have mangled you?

Cas. No.   80

Gra. I am sorry to find you thus. I have been to seek
     you.

⟨*Iago.* Lend me a garter. So. O for a chair,
To bear him easily hence!⟩

Bian. Alas! he faints! O Cassio, Cassio, Cassio!   84

Iago. Gentlemen all, I do suspect this trash
To bear a part in this.
Patience awhile, good Cassio. ⟨Come, come.⟩
Lend me a light. Know we this face, or no?   88
Alas! my friend and my dear countryman,
Roderigo? no: yes, sure. O heaven! Roderigo.

Gra. What? of Venice?

Iago. Even he, sir. Did you know him?

Gra.   Know him? ay.   92

Iago. Signior Gratiano? I cry you gentle pardon.
These bloody accidents must excuse my manners,
That so neglected you.

Gra.   I am glad to see you.

---

81 I have been to seek you; *cf. n.*
82 chair: *a plain chair, probably*
86 *Cf. n.*

Iago. How do you, Cassio? O, a chair, a chair!

Gra. Roderigo!   [*A chair brought in.*]

Iago. He. 'Tis he.—O! that's well said; the chair.
Some good man bear him carefully from hence.
I'll fetch the general's surgeon. [*To Bianca.*] For you,
  mistress,   100
Save you your labor. He that lies slain here, Cassio,
Was my dear friend. What malice was betwixt you?

Cas. None in the world; nor do I know the man.

Iago. [*To Bianca.*] What! look you pale? O, bear him
  out o' the air.   [*Cassio borne off.*]
Stay you, good gentlemen. Look you pale, mistress?—   105
Do you perceive the gastness of her eye?—
Nay, if you stare, we shall hear more anon.—
Behold her well; I pray you, look upon her.   108
Do you see, gentlemen? nay, guiltiness
Will speak though tongues were out of use.

Enter Emilia.

Emil. 'Las! what's the matter? what's the matter, husband?

Iago. Cassio has here been set on in the dark   112
By Roderigo and fellows that are 'scap'd.
He's almost slain, and Roderigo dead.

Emil. Alas, good gentleman! alas, good Cassio!

Iago. This is the fruit of whoring. Pray, Emilia,   116
Go know of Cassio where he supp'd to-night.—
What! do you shake at that?

Bian. He supp'd at my house, but I therefore shake not.

Iago. O, did he so? I charge you, go with me.

106 gastness: *ghastliness*
117 know: *learn*

Emil. Fie, fie upon thee, strumpet!   121

Bian. I am no strumpet, but of life as honest
As you that thus abuse me.

Emil.   As I! foh! fie upon thee!

Iago. Kind gentlemen, let's go see poor Cassio dress'd.
Come, mistress, you must tell's another tale.   125
Emilia, run you to the citadel,
And tell my lord and lady what has happ'd.
Will you go on afore? [*Aside.*] This is the night
That either makes me or fordoes me quite.   129

Exeunt.

SCENE SECOND

[*State Bedroom in the Citadel*]

Enter Othello with a light, and Desdemona in her bed.

Oth. It is the cause, it is the cause, my soul.
Let me not name it to you, you chaste stars!
It is the cause. Yet I'll not shed her blood,
Nor scar that whiter skin of hers than snow,   4
And smooth as monumental alablaster.
Yet she must die, else she'll betray more men.
Put out the light, and then put out the light.
If I quench thee, thou flaming minister,   8
I can again thy former light restore,
Should I repent me; but once put out thy light,
Thou cunning'st pattern of excelling nature,

126 Cf. *n.*   128 Will . . . afore; *cf. n.*
129 fordoes: *unmakes, destroys*
Scene Second S.d. Enter . . . bed; *cf. n.*
1 It is the cause; *cf. n.*   5 alablaster; *cf. n.*

I know not where is that Promethean heat   12
That can thy light relume. When I have pluck'd thy rose,
I cannot give it vital growth again.
It needs must wither. I'll smell it on the tree.

                                     He kisses her.

O balmy breath, that doth almost persuade   16
Justice to break her sword! One more, one more.
Be thus when thou art dead, and I will kill thee
And love thee after. Once more, and this the last!
So sweet was ne'er so fatal. I must weep,   20
But they are cruel tears. This sorrow's heavenly,
It strikes where it doth love. She wakes.
   Des. Who's there? Othello?
   Oth.   Ay, Desdemona.
   Des. Will you come to bed, my lord?   24
   Oth. Have you pray'd to-night, Desdemon?
   Des.   Ay, my lord.
   Oth. If you bethink yourself of any crime
Unreconcil'd as yet to heaven and grace,
Solicit for it straight.   28
   Des. Alas, my lord, what may you mean by that?
   Oth. Well, do it, and be brief. I will walk by.
I would not kill thy unprepared spirit.
No (heaven forfend!), I would not kill thy soul.   32
   Des. Talk you of killing?
   Oth.   Ay, I do.
   Des.   Then heaven
Have mercy on me!

---

12 Promethean heat: *divine fire; cf. n.*   13 relume: *rekindle*
16 doth; *cf. n.*   20 fatal; *cf. n.*
27 grace: *God's mercy*   28 Solicit: *pray*
30 by: *apart*   32 forfend: *forbid*

Oth.   Amen! with all my heart.

Des. If you say so, I hope you will not kill me.

Oth. Humh!   36

Des. And yet I fear you; for you are fatal then
When your eyes roll so. Why I should fear I know not,
Since guiltiness I know not; but yet I feel I fear.

Oth. Think on thy sins.

Des.   They are loves I bear to you.   40

Oth. Ay, and for that thou diest.

Des. That death's unnatural that kills for loving.
Alas, why gnaw you so your nether lip?
Some bloody passion shakes your very frame.   44
These are porténts, but yet, I hope, I hope,
They do not point on me.

Oth.   Peace, and be still!

Des. I will so. What's the matter?

Oth. That handkerchief which I so lov'd and gave thee
Thou gav'st to Cassio.

Des.   No, by my life and soul!   49
Send for the man and ask him.

Oth.   Sweet soul, take heed,
Take heed of perjury. Thou'rt on thy death-bed.

Des. Ay, but not yet to die.

Oth.   Yes, presently.   52
Therefore confess thee freely of thy sin;
For to deny each article with oath
Cannot remove nor choke the strong conception
That I do groan withal. Thou art to die.   56

Des. Then Lord have mercy on me!

Oth.   I say, amen.

Des. And have you mercy too! I never did

55 conception; *cf. n.*

Offend you in my life; never lov'd Cassio
But with such general warranty of heaven   60
As I might love. I never gave him token.

  Oth. By heaven, I saw my handkerchief in his hand.
O perjur'd woman! thou dost stone my heart,
And mak'st me call what I intend to do   64
A murder, which I thought a sacrifice.
I saw the handkerchief.

  Des.   He found it then.
I never gave it him. Send for him hither;
Let him confess a truth.

  Oth.   He has confess'd.   68

  Des. What, my lord?

  Oth. That he hath—uds death!

  Des.   How? unlawfully?

  Oth. Ay.

  Des.   He will not say so.

  Oth.   No; his mouth is stopp'd.
Honest Iago hath ta'en order for't.   72

  Des. O! my fear interprets. What! is he dead?

  Oth. Had all his hairs been lives, my great revenge
Had stomach for them all.

  Des. Alas, he is betray'd and I undone!   76

  Oth. O strumpet! Weep'st thou for him to my face?

  Des. O, banish me, my lord, but kill me not!

  Oth. Down, strumpet!

  Des. Kill me to-morrow; let me live to-night!   80

  Oth. Nay, an you strive,—

  Des. But half an hour!

---

60 general . . . heaven: *permission granted by heaven to all*
63 stone: *make stony*   70 *Cf. n.*
72 order: *measures*   75 stomach: *appetite*

⟨*Oth.*   Being done, there is no pause.

Des.⟩ But while I say one prayer!

Oth.   It is too late.   *He stifles her.*

«*Des.* O Lord, Lord, Lord!»   84

Emilia calls within. My lord, my lord! what, ho! my
    lord, my lord!

Oth. What noise is this? Not dead? not yet quite dead?
I that am cruel am yet merciful;
I would not have thee linger in thy pain.   88
So, so.

Emil. [*within*]. What, ho! my lord, my lord!

Oth.   Who's there?

Emil. [*within*]. O! good my lord, I'ld speak a word
    with you.

Oth. Yes; 'tis Emilia.—By and by.—She's dead.
'Tis like she comes to speak of Cassio's death.   92
The noise was high. Ha! no more moving?
Still as the grave. Shall she come in? Were't good?
I think she stirs again: no. What's the best?
If she come in, she'll sure speak to my wife: 96
My wife! my wife! what wife? I have no wife:
O, insupportable! O heavy hour!
Methinks it should be now a huge eclipse
Of sun and moon, and that the affrighted globe   100
Should yawn at alteration.

Emil. [*within*].   I do beseech you
That I may speak with you, O good my lord.

Oth. I had forgot thee. O, come in, Emilia!—

82 Being . . . pause; *cf. n.*
93 The . . . high; *cf. n.*
95 What's the best: 'what's best to do?' (Folio)
101 yawn at alteration; *cf. n.*

Soft, by and by.—Let me the curtains draw.—   104
Where art thou?   [*Unlocks the door.*]

Enter Emilia.

                    What's the matter with thee now?
Emil. O! my good lord, yonder's foul murders done.
Oth. What! now?
Emil.   But now, my lord.
Oth. It is the very error of the moon.   108
She comes more near the earth than she was wont,
And makes men mad.
Emil. Cassio, my lord, has kill'd a young Venetian
Call'd Roderigo.
Oth.   Roderigo kill'd!   112
And Cassio kill'd!
Emil.   No, Cassio is not kill'd.
Oth. Not Cassio kill'd! then murder's out of tune,
And sweet revenge grows harsh.
Des. O falsely, falsely murder'd.
Emil.   O Lord! what cry is that?   116
Oth. That? what?
Emil. Out and alas! it is my lady's voice.
Help! Help, ho! help! O lady, speak again!
Sweet Desdemona! O sweet mistress, speak!   120
Des. A guiltless death I die.
Emil. O! who has done this deed?
Des. Nobody. I myself. Farewell!
Commend me to my kind lord. O farewell!   *She dies.*
Oth. Why, how should she be murder'd?
Emil.   Alas, who knows?   125

104 Soft: *stop, wait*
107 But: *just*
                                        108 error: *aberration*

Oth. You heard her say herself it was not I.

Emil. She said so. I must needs report a truth.

Oth. She's like a liar gone to burning hell.   128
'Twas I that kill'd her.

Emil.   O the more angel she,
And you the blacker devil.

Oth. She turn'd to folly, and she was a whore.

Emil. Thou dost belie her, and thou art a devil.   132

Oth. She was false as water.

Emil.   Thou art rash as fire to say
That she was false. O she was heavenly true.

Oth. Cassio did top her. Ask thy husband else.
O I were damn'd beneath all depth in hell   136
But that I did proceed upon just grounds
To this extremity. Thy husband knew it all.

Emil. My husband?

Oth. Thy husband.   140

Emil. That she was false to wedlock?

Oth. Ay, with Cassio. Nay, had she been true,
If heaven would make me such another world
Of one entire and perfect chrysolite,   144
I'd not have sold her for it.

Emil. My husband?

Oth.   Ay, 'twas he that told me first.
An honest man he is, and hates the slime
That sticks on filthy deeds.

Emil.   My husband?   148

Oth. What needs this iterance, woman? I say thy husband.

131 folly: *unchastity*
143 such another: *another such (as large as this one)*
144 chrysolite: *a precious stone, green in color*
149 iterance: *repetition*

⟨*Emil.* O mistress! villainy hath made mocks with love.
My husband say that she was false?

    Oth.   He, woman.
I say, thy husband; dost understand the word?   **152**
My friend, thy husband, honest, honest Iago.⟩

    Emil. If he say so, may his pernicious soul
Rot half a grain a day! He lies to the heart.
She was too fond of her most filthy bargain.   **156**

    Oth. Ha!

    Emil. Do thy worst.
This deed of thine is no more worthy heaven
Than thou wast worthy her.

    Oth.   Peace! you were best.   **160**

    Emil. Thou hast not half the power to do me harm
As I have to be hurt. O gull! O dolt!
As ignorant as dirt! Thou hast done a deed,—
I care not for thy sword. I'll make thee known,   **164**
Though I lost twenty lives. Help! help, ho! help!
The Moor has kill'd my mistress! Murder! murder!

Enter Montano, Gratiano, Iago, and others.

    Mon. What is the matter? How now, general?

    Emil. O, are you come, Iago? You have done well,   **168**
That men must lay their murders on your neck.

    Gra. What is the matter?

    Emil. Disprove this villain if thou be'st a man:
He says thou told'st him that his wife was false.   **172**
I know thou didst not. Thou'rt not such a villain.
Speak, for my heart is full.

    Iago. I told him what I thought, and told no more

---

150 made mocks with: *made a dupe of*
162 gull: *fool*   170 *Gra. Cf. n.*

Than what he found himself was apt and true.   176
   Emil. But did you ever tell him she was false?
   Iago. I did.
   Emil. You told a lie, an odious damned lie;
Upon my soul, a lie, a wicked lie.   180
She false with Cassio! Did you say with Cassio?
   Iago. With Cassio, mistress. Go to, charm your tongue.
   Emil. I will not charm my tongue; I am bound to speak.
⟨My mistress here lies murder'd in her bed.   184
   All. O heavens forfend!
   Emil. And your reports have set the murder on.
   Oth. Nay, stare not, masters. It is true indeed.
   Gra. 'Tis a strange truth.   188
   Mon. O monstrous act!
   Emil.   Villainy! villainy! villainy!
I think upon't, I think, I smell't. O villainy!
I thought so then. I'll kill myself for grief.
O villainy, villainy!⟩   192
   Iago. What! are you mad? I charge you, get you home.
   Emil. Good gentlemen, let me have leave to speak.
'Tis proper I obey him, but not now.
Perchance, Iago, I will ne'er go home.   196
   Oth. Oh! Oh! Oh!   *Othello falls on the bed.*
   Emil.   Nay, lay thee down and roar,
For thou hast kill'd the sweetest innocent
That e'er did lift up eye.
   Oth.   O! she was foul.
I scarce did know you, uncle. There lies your niece,   200
Whose breath, indeed, these hands have newly stopp'd.
I know this act shows terrible and grim.

182 charm: *silence, as if by a magic spell*
191 then; *cf. n.*   196 *Cf. n.*

Gra. Poor Desdemon, I am glad thy father's dead.
Thy match was mortal to him, and pure grief   204
Shore his old thread a-twain. Did he live now,
This sight would make him do a desperate turn,
Yea, curse his better angel from his side,
And fall to reprobation.   208

Oth. 'Tis pitiful; but yet Iago knows
That she with Cassio hath the act of shame
A thousand times committed. Cassio confess'd it;
And she did gratify his amorous works   212
With the recognizance and pledge of love
Which I first gave her. I saw it in his hand.
It was a handkerchief, an antique token
My father gave my mother.   216

Emil. O God! O heavenly God!

Iago.   Zounds! hold your peace.

Emil. 'Twill out, 'twill out! I hold my peace, sir? No!
No, I will speak as liberal as the north.
Let heaven and men and devils, let them all,   220
All, all, cry shame against me, yet I'll speak.

Iago. Be wise, and get you home.

Emil.   I will not.

[*Iago threatens Emilia.*]

Gra.   Fie!
Your sword upon a woman?

Emil. O thou dull Moor! that handkerchief thou
        speak'st of   224

205 Shore: *cut*
206 do . . . turn: *commit some desperate deed*
208 reprobation: *damnation*
213 recognizance: *token*   216 *Cf. n.*
219 as . . . north: *as freely and strongly as the north wind;*
    cf. n.

I found by fortune and did give my husband,
For often with a solemn earnestness
(More than, indeed, belong'd to such a trifle)
He begg'd of me to steal it.

Iago.   Villainous whore!   228
    Emil. She give it Cassio? No, alas! I found it,
And I did give't my husband.

Iago.   Filth, thou liest!
    Emil. By heaven, I do not. I do not, gentlemen.
O murderous coxcomb! what should such a fool   232
Do with so good a wife?

Oth.   Are there no stones in heaven
But what serves for the thunder? Precious villain!

                The Moor runs at Iago. Iago kills his wife.
Gra. The woman falls. Sure, he has kill'd his wife.

                                        Exit Iago.
Emil. Ay, ay. O lay me by my mistress' side.   236
Gra. He's gone, but his wife's kill'd.
Mon. 'Tis a notorious villain. [*To Gratiano.*] Take you
    this weapon,
Which I have here recover'd from the Moor.
Come, guard the door without. Let him not pass,   240
But kill him rather. I'll after that same villain,
For 'tis a damned slave.   *Ex. Mont. and Gratiano.*

Oth.   I am not valiant neither,
But every puny whipster gets my sword.
But why should honor outlive honesty?   244
Let it go all.

233 wife; *cf. n.*   stones: *bolts; cf. n.*
239 recover'd: *taken*
243 whipster: (*cf. modern whipper-snapper*) *stripling*
244 honor: *mere dignity*   honesty: *fundamental righteousness*

Emil.   ⟨What did thy song bode, lady?
Hark, canst thou hear me? I will play the swan,
And die in music.   [*Sings.*]

                    Willow, willow, willow.   248

Moor, she was chaste. She lov'd thee, cruel Moor.
So come my soul to bliss as I speak true.
So speaking as I think, I die, I die.   *She dies.*
    Oth. I have another weapon in this chamber.   252
It is a sword of Spain, the ice brook's temper.
O here it is.—Uncle, I must come forth.
    Gra. within. If thou attempt it, it will cost thee dear.
Thou hast no weapon, and perforce must suffer.   256
    Oth. Look in upon me then, and speak to me,
Or, naked as I am, I will assault thee.

                    [*Enter Gratiano.*]

    Gra. What is the matter?
    Oth.   Behold! I have a weapon.
A better never did itself sustain   260
Upon a soldier's thigh. I have seen the day
That with this little arm and this good sword
I have made my way through more impediments
Than twenty times your stop. But O vain boast!   264
Who can control his fate? 'Tis not so now.
⟨Be not afraid, though you do see me weapon'd.
Here is my journey's end, here is my butt
And very sea-mark of my utmost sail.   268

253 ice brook's temper: *tempered in icy water*
258 naked: *unarmed (as Gratiano supposed)*
264 stop: *power of prevention*
267 butt: *goal (literally, target)*
268 sea-mark: *beacon, limit*

Do you go back dismay'd? 'Tis a lost fear.
Man but a rush against Othello's breast,
And he retires. Where should Othello go?—
Now, how dost thou look now? O ill-starr'd wench!⟩   272
Pale as thy smock! When we shall meet at compt,
This look of thine will hurl my soul from heaven,
And fiends will snatch at it. Cold, cold, my girl,
Even like thy chastity.   276
O cursed, cursed slave! Whip me, ye devils,
From the possession of this heavenly sight!
Blow me about in winds! roast me in sulphur!
Wash me in steep-down gulfs of liquid fire!   280
O Desdemona! Desdemona! dead!
O! O! O!

Enter Lodovico, Montano, Iago [prisoner], and
Officers, Cassio in a chair.

Lod. Where is this rash and most unfortunate man?
Oth. That's he that was Othello. Here I am.   284
Lod. Where is that viper? bring the villain forth.
Oth. I look down towards his feet, but that's a fable.
If that thou be'st a devil, I cannot kill thee.

                                      [Wounds Iago.]

Lod. Wring his sword from him.
Iago.   I bleed, sir, but not kill'd.   288
Oth. I am not sorry neither. I'd have thee live,
For in my sense 'tis happiness to die.

269 lost: *wasted, unnecessary*
270 Man: *wield*   rush: *bulrush, reed*
273 compt: *reckoning, on the Judgment Day*
278 possession: *haunting obsession*
286 *I look for the devil's outward sign, a cloven hoof*
288 *I bleed, sir; cf. n.*

    Lod. O thou Othello that wert once so good,
Fall'n in the practice of a damned slave,   292
What shall be said to thee?

    Oth.   Why, anything:
An honorable murderer, if you will;
For nought did I in hate, but all in honor.

    Lod. This wretch hath part confess'd his villainy. 296
Did you and he consent in Cassio's death?

    Oth. Ay.

    Cas. Dear general, I did never give you cause.

    Oth. I do believe it, and I ask you pardon.   300
Will you, I pray, demand that demi-devil
Why he hath thus ensnar'd my soul and body.

    Iago. Demand me nothing. What you know, you know:
From this time forth I never will speak word.   304

    Lod. What! not to pray?

    Gra.   Torments will ope your lips

    Oth. Well, thou dost best.

    Lod. Sir, you shall understand what hath befall'n,
Which, as I think, you know not. Here is a letter 308
Found in the pocket of the slain Roderigo,
And here another. The one of them imports
The death of Cassio to be undertook
By Roderigo.   312

    Oth. O villain!

    Cas.   Most heathenish and most gross!

    Lod. Now here's another discontented paper,
Found in his pocket too; and this, it seems,
Roderigo meant t' have sent this damned villain, 316
But that, belike, Iago in the nick

292 practice: *sinister scheme*
303 Demand me nothing; *cf. n.*   317 nick: *nick of time; cf. n.*

Came in and satisfied him.

Oth.   O the pernicious caitiff!
How came you, Cassio, by that handkerchief
That was my wife's?

Cas.   I found it in my chamber;   320
And he himself confess'd it even now
That there he dropp'd it for a special purpose
Which wrought to his desire.

Oth.   O fool! fool! fool!

Cas. There is besides in Roderigo's letter   324
How he upbraids Iago that he made him
Brave me upon the watch, whereon it came
That I was cast: and even but now he spake
(After long seeming dead): Iago hurt him,   328
Iago set him on.

Lod. You must forsake this room and go with us.
Your power and your command is taken off,
And Cassio rules in Cyprus. For this slave,   332
If there be any cunning cruelty
That can torment him much and hold him long,
It shall be his. You shall close prisoner rest,
Till that the nature of your fault be known   336
To the Venetian state. Come, bring him away.

Oth. Soft you! A word or two ⟨before you go⟩.
I have done the state some service, and they know't;
No more of that. I pray you, in your letters,   340
When you shall these unlucky deeds relate,
Speak of them as they are. Nothing extenuate,
Nor set down aught in malice. Then must you speak
Of one that lov'd not wisely but too well;   344

331 taken off: *revoked*
342 Cf. *n.*

Of one not easily jealous, but, being wrought,
Perplex'd in the extreme; of one whose hand
(Like the base Indian) threw a pearl away
Richer than all his tribe; of one whose súbdu'd eyes,   348
Albeit unused to the melting mood,
Drops tears as fast as the Arabian trees
Their méd'cinable gum. Set you down this;
And say besides, that in Aleppo once,   352
Where a malignant and a turban'd Turk
Beat a Venetian and traduc'd the state,
I took by the throat the circumcised dog,
And smote him thus.   *He stabs himself.*

  Lod. O bloody period!

  Gra.   All that's spoke is marr'd.   357

  Oth. I kiss'd thee ere I kill'd thee. No way but this,
Killing myself to die upon a kiss.   *He dies.*

  Cas. This did I fear, but thought he had no weapon;
For he was great of heart.

  Lod.   [*To Iago.*] O Spartan dog,   361
More fell than anguish, hunger, or the sea,
Look on the tragic loading of this bed!
This is thy work. The object poisons sight;   364
Let it be hid. Gratiano, keep the house,
And seize upon the fortunes of the Moor,

345 wrought: *wrought upon, worked up*
346 Perplex'd: *desperately troubled*
347 Indian; *cf. n.*
351 méd'cinable; *cf. n.*
352 Aleppo; *cf. n.*
357 period: *ending, close*
361 Spartan: *for fierceness and taciturnity*
362 fell: *deadly*
365 Let it be hid; *cf. n.*
366 seize upon: *take legal possession of*

For they succeed to you. To you, lord governor,
Remains the censure of this hellish villain,   368
The time, the place, the torture. O, enforce it!
Myself will straight aboard, and to the state
This heavy act with heavy heart relate.   *Exeunt omnes.*

367 succeed: *descend in succession* (*as nearest relative of Des-
    demona*)
369 enforce it: *make it severe*

FINIS.

NOTES

AT *the time of his sudden death in June of 1946, Professor Brooke had com-pleted his work on the text, notes, and glosses for Hamlet, King Lear, Othello and I Henry IV. The editorial tasks which he left unfinished—preparation of some of the final copy for the press, reading of the proofs, compilation of the Indexes of Words Glossed, decisions as to certain matters of style and format, and, in the case of I Henry IV, the rescuing of the text from the prescriptive punctuation of the eighteenth-century editors—have been undertaken by Pro-fessor Benjamin Nangle.*

TEXTUAL NOTE. The two authorities for the text of *Othello* are the first separate (quarto) edition, printed in 1622, and the version included in the first collected (folio) edition of Shakespeare's dramatic works, published in 1623. Neither is based directly on the other, though there is some indication that both go back to a common manuscript authority which itself was a deriva-tive from Shakespeare's original. The Quarto text is the shorter by more than 150 lines. These lines (missing in Quarto 1, but nearly all restored in the second Quarto of 1630) are here printed within angle brackets (⟨ ⟩). Some of these (*e.g.,* IV.i.175–177, V.ii.266–272) are clearly accidental omissions; others have the appearance of stage cuts. The much less numerous passages which appear in the first Quarto, but not in the Folio, are here printed within ornamental brackets (« »).

Neither of the 'substantive' texts of *Othello* can be said to be well printed. Each has a rather high proportion of plain typographical error, and there are some passages where a tolerable reading can be secured only by blend-ing what appears to be authentic in either the Quarto or the Folio and ejecting the faults of both. In other places variants are found which are so nearly balanced in merit that it is hard to say which word Shakespeare really wrote. In such conditions it is unlikely that a perfectly scientific and satisfactory edition of *Othello* will ever be produced. However, when the faults of the Quarto are weighed against those of the Folio, it becomes quite certain that the margin of virtue is on the side of the former; and this means, since the early editors had a strong prejudice in favor of the Folio, that a considerable number of readings have had to be eliminated in the present edition which familiarity has endeared, but which reason can no longer justify.

The Quarto marks the act divisions, except Act III. The Folio divides the play correctly into both acts and scenes (with a slight deviation from modern practice at II.iii) and adds 'The Names of the Actors' on the last page. The stage directions are fuller in the Quarto, and these have generally been followed; a very few have been taken from the second Quarto of 1630. Necessary amplifications and other essential matter omitted in the original editions are supplied within square brackets.

In Shakespeare's usage it was optional to give full syllabic value to the ending *-ed* of past verbal forms or (as is generally done now) to contract this ending with the preceding syllable. In the present edition final *-ed* must always be pronounced as a separate syllable in order to preserve the original rhythm of the verse. Where rhythm requires the contracted form, the spelling *'d* is used.

Shakespeare accented a number of words on syllables which do not now bear the accent, and sometimes his practice in this matter was inconsistent. Where an unusual accentuation is required, it is indicated by an acute mark over the stressed vowel, as in *séquester*.

Obsolete words and words employed in now unusual senses are explained in footnotes the first time they occur in the text. Repetitions are not usually noted and when they occur should be sought in the *Index of Words Glossed* at the end of the volume.

The critical and general notes in the present section are announced by the symbol, *cf. n.*, at the bottom of the page of text to which each has relevance. A name at the end of a note (in parentheses) indicates the authority; but no special effort is made to give credit for material which is common property or which is, so far as known, new in the present edition.

I.i.4. *'Sblood.* An oath, contracted from 'God's blood'; as *'Zounds,* line 86 below, is a contraction from 'God's wounds,'—the reference in both cases being to Christ (as of one substance with God) on the cross. In 1606 King James I caused an Act to be passed forbidding blasphemy on the stage, and accordingly these oaths are omitted in the Folio edition of the play, while other similar expressions throughout are either omitted or softened; cf. Iago's mild ejaculation in IV.i.144.

I.i.8. *Three great ones.* Three quite mythical characters. Iago was never an open candidate for the office of lieutenant. Neither Othello, Cassio, nor Emilia knows of such a thing, and Iago does not mention it again. He invents this story in order to disarm Roderigo's suspicion that he has been preferring Othello's interests to Roderigo's. (It may be, in spite of line 7, that Iago's vague distaste for Othello first crystallizes into conscious hate at this moment, when he starts inventing specious reasons for it.)

I.i.13. *bombast circumstance.* Bombast was a cheap kind of cotton stuff used for padding Elizabethan garments; the obvious metaphorical use was very common.

I.i.20. *Florentine.* Iago sneers at Cassio's place of origin because the name connotes what 'Parisian' or 'Bostonian' might.

I.i.21. *A fellow almost damn'd in a fair wife.* Properly punctuated by the Folio as a parenthetical remark. Cassio, says Iago, is a fellow of such effeminate quality that the like could hardly be endured in a fine lady. Here *in* means 'in the person of' and *wife* 'woman' in general. In this description of Cassio Iago is again lying (compare note on II.iii.130) in order to build up

Roderigo's belief that Othello has misused him. The obscure feeling called inferiority complex drives him in the same direction. It is evident that Shakespeare had confidence in the ability of the actor of Iago, who thus begins his role with two statements that the audience must not be allowed to accept with the full faith Roderigo gives them. (The name of the first impersonator of Iago has not been recorded. In the following generation Joseph Taylor [c. 1586–1653], who also played Hamlet, was famous in the part.)

I.i.30. *belee'd and calm'd.* A nautical metaphor, meaning 'Have the wind (of Othello's favor) taken from my sails: be superseded by this interloper.'

I.i.31. *Debitor-and-Creditor.* A coined name of contempt for Cassio: 'Mr. Bookkeeper.' *counter-caster.* 'One who casts accounts, or reckons by counters'; cf. Iago's earlier term, *arithmetician,* line 19 above. These expressions are all intended to cast contempt on Cassio as a man of books and figures, not of warlike deeds. They are later shown to be contrary to fact, except in that Cassio did apparently possess technical qualifications which Iago lacked.

I.i.33. *God bless the mark!* Originally this was a pious formula to avert the consequences of an evil omen; then, by ironical inversion, it came to be a contemptuous interjection equivalent to 'forsooth' or a mild oath. *ancient.* This spelling represents the way in which the word 'ensign' was pronounced. Cassio and Iago were of higher rank than their titles indicate, for they were staff-officers, the commander-in-chief's immediate aides.

I.i.39. *in any . . . affin'd.* The image is from the old tables or terms of affinity which controlled legal marriage and were posted in churches. Do I stand, asks Iago, in any such close spiritual relationship with the Moor that it is my duty to love him?

I.i.68. *Rouse him.* Like the other pronouns in this line, *him* must refer to Othello, not Brabantio. No actor could read the line adequately otherwise.

I.i.86. *For shame . . . gown!* Iago is simply enjoying this exhibition of the senator in *negligé.*

I.i.115–117. *your daughter . . . two backs.* Borrowed from Rabelais (Bk. I, ch. 3).

I.i.118. *a senator.* Iago, who belongs to the left politically, and who is exploiting his advantage in being unknown, implies that in answering 'Villain!' with 'Senator!' one is offering a generous *quid pro quo.*

I.i.123. The tedious time about midnight; a 'toss-up,' indeterminate odd or even, as to whether it be the last moments of one day or the first of the next.

I.i.136. *extravagant and wheeling.* There is a reference here to Othello's being a 'soldier of fortune,' not a native of Venice. Venetian law required that the commander-in-chief of Venetian forces should be a politically disqualified alien, so that no political ambition might distract him from the strict performance of his military duties and jeopardize the security of the state.

I.i.150. *Cyprus wars.* The historical date at which the action of the play took place has usually been given as 1570, on the strength of Reed's assertion that in that year 'Mustapha, Selymus' general, attacked Cyprus,' after having effected a junction with another Turkish fleet at Rhodes. But in the play (1) the Turks did not 'attack' Cyprus, and (2) they were reported (I.iii.14–31) as intending to 'attack' Rhodes—which had been in their hands since 1522. The date of the action of the play must therefore be placed between 1471, the year in which the Venetians assumed virtual sovereignty of Cyprus, and 1522, the year in which the Turks became masters of Rhodes. The Turkish expedition described in the play must then have been either too abortive for record in history or entirely fictitious, for none such is known between those dates according to Malone and Reed (Furness, 357); but the 'hypothetical attack' cited in Appendix A (1) as 'meditated, according to report' in 1508 (Furness, 374) would satisfy all Shakespeare's requirements.

I.i.158. *the Sagittary.* 'The Sign of the Archer.' Most likely an inn in the neighborhood of the famous Venetian Arsenal.

I.i.163. *unhappy.* Hapless, ill-fated, unfortunate; cf. III.iv.100.

I.ii.5. *him.* Evidently Brabantio, as is made clear in Iago's next speech (line 12 ff.). He has been giving Othello a highly spiced account of Brabantio's comments on the wedding. (Iago never talks of his association with Roderigo.)

I.ii.13,14. 'And has, in actual effect (though not by law), an influence as weighty as the Duke's own.' Iago was simply 'talking big' in order to alarm Othello by exaggerating Brabantio's importance.

I.ii.23. *speak unbonneted.* Speak on equal terms, without removing the hat as one did in the presence of a superior. 'Uncapped' could be used in the same way. In *Coriolanus*, II.ii.30, *bonneted* has the contrary sense, having hats off in token of humility.

Notes

I.ii.26. *unhoused*. Possibly merely 'unmarried'; but probably 'un-hampered,' free as the open air; just the opposite of 'cabin'd, cribb'd, confin'd,' *Macbeth* III.iv.24.

I.ii.33 S.d. *Enter Cassio with lights, Officers and torches*. Perhaps in two groups, each with lights. The emphasis on lighting effects in this scene may indicate that it was meant to be acted indoors at court. A type of drama popular at this period was commonly known as the 'nocturnal' (see W. J. Lawrence, 'Shakespeare from a New Angle,' *Studies*, Dublin, Sept., 1919).

I.ii.51. *lawful prize*. Iago uses metaphors from buccaneering. Desdemona is a *land*-carrack (cf. 'prairie schooner'), and Othello's problem is that of the Elizabethan privateer: Will the prize-court allow him to keep his booty?

I.ii.52. *I do not understand*. Contrast III.iii.70 ff., 94 ff. Presumably Cassio, who is punctilious, does not understand himself to be at liberty to avow what he knows.

I.ii.53. *Marry*. The word, originally an oath or ejaculation calling on the Virgin Mary, is here used by Iago to create a pun. For its use as a simple ejaculation, cf. II.iii.262, III.i.10.

I.ii.98,99. If Othello is allowed to commit such an outrage with impunity, Venice may just as well give up the caste system.

I.iii.S.d. *Enter . . . Attendants*. A typical stage direction. The characters do not literally enter, but are revealed by drawing the curtain of the rear stage.

I.iii.10–12. I do not feel so reassured by the mere discrepancy in detail as not to credit, with dreadful apprehensions, the under-lying main point.

I.iii.46. *Write from us, etc.* Command him in our name to use the greatest haste (the Quarto reading).

I.iii.61. *mountebanks*. Brabantio's charge, which he has been gradually elaborating (cf. I.i.171 ff., I.ii.72 ff.), now expresses itself in the language Laertes had used in *Hamlet* IV.iii.140.

I.iii.67–69. *the bloody book of law . . . sense*. Capital punishment shall be imposed according to your own interpretation of the bitter letter of the law.

I.iii.76 ff. For discussion of Shakespeare's use of the oration as a branch of rhetoric see M. B. Kennedy, *The Oration in Shakespeare* (1942).

I.iii.95. *motion*. Desdemona was so still and pure by nature that she couldn't move without blushing.

I.iii.139. *portance . . . history*. These adventures of Othello are closely paralleled by those related in Captain John Smith's

True Travels, Adventures and Observations (1630). When the play was written Smith had not yet gone to Virginia, but he had suffered all the vicissitudes Othello here mentions.

I.iii.144. *Anthropophagi, etc.* For Shakespeare's information about these creatures see J. Milton French, 'Othello among the Anthropophagi,' *PMLA*, Sept., 1934.

I.iii.166. *Upon this heat.* The Quarto reading. The Folio substitute, 'Upon this *hint*,' has required so much defence that readers have grown fond of it, but it is probably a scribal or typographical slip occasioned by recollection of line 142, 'It was my hint to speak.' It is unlikely that Shakespeare would employ so banal a phrase twice in twenty-five lines, particularly in a passage of such high finish.

I.iii.202–219. These staccato riming couplets are introduced, as prose is later, for contrast and orchestral effect. After a great movement in blank verse, which is the idiom of youth, romance, and passion, Shakespeare brings in the balanced rime, which is the idiom of age, caution, and experience. The same means are employed in *Romeo and Juliet* as the balcony scene (II.ii) is linked to the scene (II.iii) at Friar Lawrence's cell.

I.iii.205. *more mischief.* Quarto reading. The Folio has 'new mischief.' There are many cases like this in *Othello*, where the merits of the two texts are so closely balanced that an editor must be content to impute to Shakespeare what his own taste selects as slightly the more euphonious or more meaningful.

I.iii.206,207. Part of the art of the gnomic couplet lay in confusion of the prose order of words. The sense here is: When Fortune takes what cannot be preserved, Patience makes a mockery of Fortune's injury.

I.iii.216,217. *to sugar . . . sides.* Having converse and opposed powers, capable of either sweetening or embittering.

I.iii.220. In the Folio this line is recast in the form of prose. Shakespeare may so have written or rewritten it to serve as a transition to the Duke's speech which follows.

I.iii.256. *A moth of peace.* A concentrated metaphor. It suggests the futile fluttering of a moth, its confined sphere indoors, and its triviality; while there is also a kind of pun on Desdemona 'fretting' like a moth in the midst of peace.

I.iii.264. *distinct.* Both the early texts here read 'defunct,' and the obscurity resulting has led to some of the most repellent emendations in the Shakespeare canon. In Elizabethan script 'distinct' and 'defunct' are very similar. Shakespeare is notably fond of the word *distinct* in the present sense of 'separate,' 'individual.' The sense of the passage has been further obscured for modern readers by two Elizabethanisms in the previous line: the omission of the relative after *heat*, and the 'Northern' verbal plural in *affects*, both quite characteristic of Shakespeare.

I.iii.269. *seel*. Folio reading; Quarto 'foyles.' Literally, a hawking term, meaning to sew the lids of a falcon's eyes together in order to restrict the sight while the bird was being trained; thence used metaphorically in a variety of senses, such as to blind, cover, conceal, restrain.

I.iii.270. *speculative and offic'd*. The inferior reading of the Quarto, 'speculative and active,' is interesting. It suggests that someone (probably not Shakespeare) was thinking of the old mediaeval coupling of contemplative and active.

I.iii.279. *ten*. No one is likely ever to know whether Shakespeare set the hour for *ten*, as the Quarto says, or 'nine' as the Folio has it. Perhaps he used a Roman numeral, 'x' or 'ix.' Compare *King Lear*, I.ii.176.

I.iii.292,293. It is again optional to prefer the Quarto version:
Look to her, Moor! Have a quick eye to see.
She has deceiv'd her father, may do thee.

I.iii.386–389. *it is . . . surety*. The author's purpose is not to discredit Emilia or Othello, who are clearly innocent, but to show that Iago (unlike Othello) has a morbidly jealous nature and is morbidly seeking to rationalize the obscure hostility he feels.

I.iii.393. *double knavery*. Referring to the two purposes mentioned in the preceding line: to get Cassio's place and *plume up* (pamper) Iago's injured ego. Iago, whose reputation for 'honesty' revolts him as a reflection on his intellect, finds a real solace in picturing himself as a clever knave.

II.i.S.d. The place, not definitely mentioned, is evidently Famagosta, which the Turks captured after a famous siege that lasted from 1569 till 1571. The time is a Saturday afternoon (cf. III.iii.60f.) something over a week (cf. II.i.77) after the close of Act I.

II.i.3. *'twixt the haven and the main*. Between the harbor and the point where the sea fades into the horizon. Folio reading: ''twixt the Heauen, and the Maine.'

II.i.26. *La Veronesa*. The early texts have 'A Veronessa' ('A Verennessa'), probably a copyist's or printer's misreading.

II.i.50,51. Therefore, while not foolishly over-confident, I am emboldened to hope for the best. A condensed figure almost incapable of precise literal paraphrase.

II.i.51. *Messenger.* The Folio dispenses with the Messenger, making this speech an off-stage cry and assigning his subsequent speech to one of the gentlemen already on the stage. Throughout this scene, the Quarto and Folio texts are frequently at variance in the stage directions and assignment of speeches to the various characters, reflecting the difficulties of the early producers in coping with the complicated action and crowded stage. The present text generally follows the Quarto, which here, as elsewhere, gives more thoughtful attention to these details.

II.i.65. *ingen-giver.* What Shakespeare here wrote has bothered all editors, and evidently bothered the earliest printers. The Folio, attempting to follow copy, produces a nonsense word: 'Do's tyre the Ingeniuer.' The Quarto evades the issue by inventing a flat paraphrase: 'Does beare all excellency.' The suggested emendations of earlier editors have read little sense into the passage. The present reading, assuming that the Folio compositor, faced with utterly illegible copy, dropped a 'g' from the word, renders the sentence plausible. *Ingen* (ingine, engine; Latin *ingenium*) meant native talent, mother wit, the mental and moral qualities which come from nature rather than art, and in Platonic conception belong to the inner rather than the outer beauty. The word in this sense was common in Elizabethan and Jacobean literature, and was even used for the names of characters who, like Ingen in Nathan Field's *Amends for Ladies* (c. 1612), represented

> 'The fountain of humanity, the prize
> Of every virtue, moral and divine:'

In the present passage (as in Field's) the *ingen-giver* is Nature who by Cassio's image tires herself by the multitude of her benefactions to Desdemona. Lines 64, 65 laud her beauty of soul, as lines 62, 63 do her outward beauty. Cassio was a Florentine, and thereby something of a Platonist.

II.i.95. *So . . . news.* Alternative readings of Quarto and Folio respectively. Each satisfactorily completes the metrical line.

II.i.112. *housewifery, housewives.* Pronounced 'huzzifry,' 'huzzivs.' The modern 'hussy' (merely a phonetic transcription of 'housewife') shows the slur intended.

II.i.155. Probably some cant saying or 'double entendre' gave point to this line in Shakespeare's day.

II.i.169,170. *I . . . courtship.* The Quarto has 'I will catch you in your own courtesies,' and above (168 f.) '. . . whisper: as little a web as this will ensnare as great a Flee as Cassio.'

II.i.201. *set down the pegs,* etc. Iago develops the musical image suggested by Othello in *discords* (line 198).

II.i.243. *A subtle, slippery knave.* Folio: 'A slipper and subtle knave.' In these prose speeches the two texts exhibit a number of slight variations. The Folio may contain actors' additions. (Note the words in angle brackets.)

II.i.278. *taste.* The first Quarto reading, 'trust,' may be right.

II.i.284. *if you can.* Most editors here read with the Quarto 'if I can'; but the Folio is correct. It is Iago who makes the opportunities.

II.i.306,307. *whom . . . hunting.* 'Whom I flog to make him hunt faster.' The reference is to beating an ill-trained dog to make him more diligent. Instead of *thrash,* the first Quarto reads 'crush,' the second and the Folio 'trace'; but these yield no tolerable sense, and it seems evident that Roderigo is called 'trash of Venice' only for the sake of a pun.

II.i.307. *stand the putting on.* That is, if Roderigo doesn't break down under the rigor of my discipline. One sense of 'put on' was to lay a hound on the scent (*O.E.D.*, Put 46. 1).

II.ii.6. *addiction.* So the second Quarto (1630). This may be Shakespeare's word, but if so was a very early use of it and was not understood by the printer of either the first Quarto (who substitutes 'mind') or the Folio (who spells it 'addition').

II.ii.10. *tolled.* Both Quartos and the Folio read 'told.' See H. Kökeritz, 'Two Sets of Shakespearean Homophones,' *R.E.S.,* Oct., 1943.

II.iii. No new scene was necessary here on the Elizabethan stage, and none is indicated in the Folios or Quartos. Theobald first assigned a new location for the action after the Herald's departure, and Capell first added the caption 'Scene iii.'

II.iii.29. *Well,* etc. Iago gives up the effort to lure Cassio into indiscreet comment on the general's wife.

II.iii.56. *hold their honors in a wary distance.* Are skittish about them; allow none to approach too close.

II.iii.62. *If consequence do but approve my dream.* If the outcome only justifies my hope.

II.iii.68. This song like the next (line 89) need not be credited to Iago's invention. The first was quite possibly an Elizabethan tavern catch, and the second is a mélange of old ballads.

II.iii.130. *He'll watch the horologe a double set.* He'll see the hour-hand of the clock make two complete revolutions; *i.e.,* stay awake for twenty-four hours at a stretch. Iago is expert at adjusting his prevarications to what the traffic will bear. To the civilian Roderigo, in I.i., he can safely picture Cassio as a military nincompoop; to the commander Montano, who doubtless knows Cassio's professional reputation but not his personal habits, he can safely deplore the fact that Cassio is a dipsomaniac, while belauding his military competence.

II.iii.148. *twiggen* (Quarto 'wicker') *bottle.* Either 'slash him till he resembles a Chianti bottle covered with straw net-work' (Booth), or 'beat him till he runs to hide himself in one of the wicker flasks we've just been using' (Hart). Cf. also *Much Ado About Nothing* I.i.267: 'Hang me in a bottle like a cat And shoot at me,' and the note thereon.

II.iii.162. *Diablo.* Oath or exclamation of excitement: 'the Devil!' A typical Jacobean affectation of elegance was this garnishing of the speech with scraps of Spanish.

II.iii.168. *all sense of place and duty.* Since Quarto and Folio agree in the misarrangement, 'all place of sense and duty,' it looks as if both were based on a common source.

II.iii.172. *Which heaven has forbid the Ottomites.* That is, heaven has, through the storm, forbidden the Turks to kill us.

II.iii.217. *on . . . safety.* Guard-post established to secure the general safety. Hendiadys for 'court of guard' (cf. II.i.218).

II.iii.306. *Hydra.* A monster with nine heads. Whenever one was cut off, several new ones replaced it. The destruction of the Lernæan Hydra was the second of the Twelve Labors of Hercules.

II.iii.350 f. *this parallel course Directly to his good.* This course which runs straight in line with his advantage.

III.i.2.S.d. *Clown.* The Clown here must have been a licensed jester, like Touchstone, in Othello's train; cf. III.iv.1–23. (This stage direction comes from the second Quarto.)

III.i.3,4. The Neapolitans spoke Italian with a marked nasal twang.

III.i.41. Iago was a Venetian, Cassio a Florentine. The latter merely means to say, 'I never experienced more honesty and kindness even in one of my own countrymen than in this man' (Malone).

III.i.50. Opportunity, in the fable, had no hair on the back of the head and hence must be grasped by the forelock.

III.ii.2. *state.* The Folio has 'Senate.'

III.iii.14–16. 'He may either of himself think it politic to keep me out of office so long, or he may be satisfied with such slight reasons, or so many accidents may' arise to postpone from time

Notes

to time his intended re-instatement of me, 'that I may be quite forgotten' (Johnson).

III.iii.23. *watch him tame.* A metaphor drawn from falconry. Hawks were tamed, *i.e.,* their fierce spirit of resistance was broken, by deprivation of sleep.

III.iii.60. *to-morrow . . . morn.* This tells us that the day is Sunday and that the arrival in Cyprus occurred on Saturday. The last four acts of this tragedy cover about thirty-six hours.

III.iii.92. *Chaos is come again.* The most emphatic of assurances. I love you, and will till the world returns to chaos. Thus ends in utter failure the plan Iago outlined in the closing lines of Act II for arousing Othello's jealousy.

III.iii.94. *Did Michael Cassio . . . Know of your love?* Thus Iago starts again, building, as his manner is, on the new fact he has just picked up.

III.iii.127. *seem none.* 'No longer seem, or bear the shape of men' (Johnson).

III.iii.149. *conjects.* A very good word, replaced in the Folio by the commoner 'conceits.' This whole speech is here printed as in the Quarto, which seems to give the earlier version. Note that in lines 93–154 Iago is implying nothing about Desdemona, but is playing on Othello's urgent official need to learn the truth about Cassio's trustworthiness, which had been so strangely impugned by the events of the night before (cf. II. iii.247 ff.).

III.iii.156. *our souls.* The Quarto reading, which seems more authentic than the Folio 'their souls.' In this speech Iago begins slyly to turn his insinuations toward Desdemona, but the speech is merely his ingenious parody of Cassio on reputation (II.iii.263 ff.).

III.iii.171. *O misery!* An objective, not subjective, exclamation. It means 'How intolerable!', and is the comment of a sensitive outsider upon the horrid picture Iago is painting. In line 176 Othello bursts into astonished outcry on perceiving that he is himself being linked with jealousy.

III.iii.182. *exsufflicate.* A coined word, not instanced elsewhere, but a good one. 'Exsufflate' would be normal.

III.iii.260–263. An elaborate metaphor drawn from falconry. A *haggard* was a wild hawk caught when mature and often found to be irreclaimable, unamenable to discipline. A word with such a meaning readily lent itself to use as a term of reproach for a loose woman. *Jesses* were leather leg-straps by which the hawk was fastened to the leash. 'The falconers always let the hawk fly [*whistle her off* = start her] against the wind; if she flies with the wind behind her, she seldom returns. If therefore a hawk was for any reason to be dismissed, she was "let down the wind," and from that time shifted for herself and "preyed at fortune"' (Johnson).

III.iii.286. *your head.* The Folio substitutes 'it hard,' perhaps because 'yr' (your) in the manuscript was read as 'yt' (it).

III.iii.292. *a hundred times.* One of the numerous hints at the lapse of a considerable amount of time which are dropped in this part of the play to counteract the impression of melodramatic and improbable haste. See note on III.iv.171.

III.iii.306. *handkerchief.* Spelled 'handkercher' always in Quarto, and that was probably Shakespeare's form.

III.iii.355. *wide throats.* Folio: 'rude throats.' In this most famous scene the old prestige of the Folio text sometimes adds the charm of familiarity to the less defensible reading. It is necessary to distinguish between what Shakespeare probably wrote and what Kean and Booth declaimed. *Wide throats* and in the next line *great clamor* (Folio 'dread Clamours') better suit the context and Othello's dignity. The Folio variants suggest that even by 1623 the language of the great speeches had suffered here and there from stagy heightening. (But 'rude' may be an honest misreading of the same manuscript word as *wide*.)

III.iii.386. *Her name.* This reading, *Her*, is based on the second Quarto, correcting 'My' in the Folio. The passage is not in the first Quarto.

III.iii.429. The Folio assigns this line to Othello.

III.iii.440. *any that.* Malone's emendation for 'any, it' in the early texts. In Elizabethan handwriting *yt* was commonly used for both 'that' and 'it.'

III.iii.453–460. Steevens cites Holland's translation of Pliny's *Natural History*, 1601, as the probable source of Shakespeare's assertion about the current of the Pontic or Black Sea (the ancient Pontus Euxinus). The first Quarto omits the passage.

III.iv.46,47. The commentators have brought to light sufficient early plays on the words 'hearts' and 'hands' (to which might be added Herrick's *Panegerick* to Sir Lewis Pemberton, lines 35–43) to show that this was a favorite quibble. The meaning is: The joining of hands in marriage formerly meant the giving of hearts also, but nowadays we have a formal outward union of hands without any accompanying inward union of hearts.

III.iv.51. *sorry rheum.* The Quarto has 'sullen rhume,' which may be right.

III.iv.76. *Most veritable.* Said ironically, no doubt. Othello is inventing marvels about the handkerchief to try his wife's conscience. Compare V.ii.212 ff.

III.iv.100. *I am most unhappy in the loss of it.* The admirable Emilia has been unfairly blamed for not confessing the theft of the handkerchief. The next lines explain. Emilia loves and fears and (like everybody else) fundamentally trusts Iago. She has the generous trait of imputing her husband's trying qualities to the general imperfection of men, and has not been depressed to see the great Othello behave in as childish a manner (lines 33–96). She thinks him irritated over the temporary loss of a keepsake, and there is nothing in the situation as she understands it which would oblige her at this point to violate Iago's confidence, disobey his command (III.iii.319), and arouse his anger. Jealousy in her view is a totally irrational passion (lines 157–160) and not worth too much bother.

III.iv.171. *keep a week away.* This passage, Lodovico's arrival with the message from the Senators presupposing their receipt of a report from Othello about the Turks' discomfiture (IV.i. 216 ff.), Roderigo's 'Every day thou daffest me' (IV.ii.176), and various other points in the play would seem to imply that many days must have elapsed since Othello's arrival in Cyprus; yet an unbroken sequence of time-indications can be cited to show that he landed Saturday afternoon and killed Desdemona Sunday night. In this dilemma (which arises, of course, only in close study of the play, never in witnessing a performance) John Wilson ('Christopher North') in 1850 proposed the theory that Shakespeare consciously or unconsciously employed 'Double Time,' *i.e.*, Dramatic or Short Time and Historic or Long Time: 'Short for maintaining the tension of the passion, Long for a thousand general needs; . . . one for our sympathy with Othello's tempest of heart, one for the verisimilitude of the transaction.' Every playwright does something of the sort, but the method in *Othello* is particularly bold.

IV.i.17. *They have it very oft that have it not.* People often have honor (receive outward respect) who have no honor (possess no inward virtue).

IV.i.19. *I would most gladly have forgot it.* The purpose of Iago's gross talk now appears. In the brief interval since Othello left the stage (III.iv.96), his normal balance has begun to re-assert itself and the slanders have taken on unreality. Iago finds himself in a position of direst peril, and for the moment escapes by so nauseating his victim as to deprive him of the use of his reason.

IV.i.35–44. These are the disjointed ejaculations of an agonized mind on the verge of collapse. There are few phrases in it where the reference is not fairly clear.

IV.i.89,90. *all . . . man*. Altogether given over to mere passionate impulse, and not a real man.

IV.i.110. This line and all Othello's speeches down to line 170 are supposed to be spoken in his hiding-place, where he is both visible and audible to the audience, but neither visible nor audible to Cassio and Iago.

IV.i.175–177. The omission of this speech in the first Quarto was clearly accidental. That the printer had Iago's speech in his copy is shown by the fact that Othello's preceding speech, which comes at the bottom of a page, is followed by the catchword 'Iag.' Iago's speech is then dropped out, the next page beginning with Othello's subsequent speech. The second Quarto also omits Iago's speech, running Othello's two speeches into one.

IV.i.196. *the pity of it, Iago, etc.* The longer version of this speech in the Folio may be an actor's amplification.

IV.i.207. *Strangle her.* If poison were used, Iago would be an accomplice, and there might be no way to convict Othello of the crime. Moreover, Iago nowhere shows any malice against Desdemona. He may think Othello incapable of strangling her and may mean to give her a chance of life.

IV.i.228. *This fail you not to do, etc.* The regular formula for closing formal orders: 'This fail you not to do, as you will enjoy our favor,' or ' . . . as you will answer to us for any disobedience.'

IV.ii.47. *they.* The Quartos read 'he.' Perhaps Shakespeare wrote 'God' for *heaven* in line 46 and withdrew it as over-bold.

IV.ii.53,54. This noble image seems to be printed correctly in the first Quarto. The Folio somewhat garbles it:

'The fixed Figure for the time of Scorne,
   To point his slow, and mouing finger at,'

and the commentators have garbled it still more. Othello pictures himself as one of the figures on the dial of Scorn's clock, pointed at by Scorn's two hands or 'fingers,'—fingers which move so slowly as not to seem to move at all, and yet move through all eternity.

IV.ii.56–59. Dr. Johnson very strangely objected to this masterly pair of metaphors, the grain-garner and the fountain, elemental food and drink, the two sustaining principles represented by Desdemona, without which Othello cannot live.

IV.ii.61,62. *Turn . . . cherubin.* Look on that sight and blush! Young and rose-lipped Patience at such a spectacle will become a fire-red cherub.

IV.ii.62. *cherubin.* A plural form used with a singular signification, by a common mistake. That the cherub was traditionally painted with a scarlet countenance is vouched for by Chaucer's phrase, 'a fyr-reed cherubinnes face' (*Prologue*, 624).

IV.ii.63. *I here look grim as hell.* A bleak and tortured line, not to be improved by emendation. Here I stand, says Othello, so unl:ke the cherubim, so black and desperate.

IV.ii.66. *quicken . . . blowing.* The reference is to the blow-fly, which lays its eggs on meat—*cf.* shambles—and 'again becomes pregnant [quicken] the very instant it has laid a batch of eggs [blowing]' (Deighton).

IV.ii.67,68. *O thou black weed . . . sweet.* Quarto reading. The Folio, perhaps in an (imperfect) effort to divide the lines evenly, reads:

> 'O thou weed:
> Who art so lovely fair, and smell'st so sweet.'

It remains beautiful, but something precious has been lost.

IV.ii.80,81. *What . . . strumpet.* These four words, of which the last two are not in the Folio, look like an insertion. If they are omitted, the words before and after form a perfect line.

IV.ii.135. *Fie! there is no such man.* Not a shallow lie, probably, but Iago's confession to himself that mere self-interest would not account for what he is doing.

IV.ii.182. Compare I.i.4. The situation here is very much as at the opening of the play.

IV.ii.226. *Mauritania.* It is on such expressions as this and Iago's 'Barbary' (I.i.111) that those rely who wish to prove that Shakespeare thought of Othello as a bronze-colored Moor, while those who maintain that he conceived of him as a jet-black full-blooded negro cite I.i.66, I.ii.70, III.iii.387,388, etc. Ignorantly or by intention, Shakespeare has combined distinct ethnic traits to produce the blend of romance and realism that the tragedy called for. (There is no reason to believe that Othello is, as Iago says, returning to Mauritania.)

IV.iii.1. After supper they have been showing Lodovico the living quarters in the Citadel. He is now about to leave.

IV.iii.29. *An old thing 'twas.* As this indicates, the famous 'willow song' which follows was not original with Shakespeare. It was perhaps first written (for a man) by John Heywood, 'the Epigrammatist,' in the reign of Henry VIII. A version exists with Elizabethan music.

IV.iii.106. Not to be corrupted by bad example, but take it as a warning.

V.i.14. *Every way makes my gain.* Wishful thinking. Nothing would now save Iago but for Cassio and Roderigo each neatly to eliminate the other, and nobody ask intelligent questions afterwards.

V.i.19. *a daily beauty in his life.* This shows the collapse of Iago's philosophy. The only daily beauty in Cassio's life is the beauty of loyal devotion to his commander, over which Iago had made so merry in I.i.43 ff.

V.i.27 S.d. *Enter Othello.* He has seen Lodovico to his lodging and is returning.

V.i.81. *I have been to seek you.* This presumably accounts for Gratiano's absence at the opening of IV.iii.

V.i.86. *To bear a part in this.* So the Quarto. The Folio reads 'To be a party in this injury,' which scans, but is certainly weak.

V.i.126. *Emilia, run you to the citadel.* Iago's purpose here is debatable. Did he wish Emilia to intervene in time to save Desdemona's life? Did he wish her message to shame Othello into a murder he might not otherwise commit?

V.i.128. *Will . . . afore?* Addressed to the 'kind gentlemen' of line 124. The purpose is to leave Iago for a moment alone on the stage. (The Quarto printer did not understand *afore* and substituted 'I pray.')

V.ii.S.d. *Enter . . . bed.* Phrased as in second Quarto (less full in first Quarto and Folio). On the Elizabethan stage Othello would enter and, drawing the curtain before the rear stage, under the balcony, reveal Desdemona in bed asleep.

V.ii.1. *It is the cause.* Probably explained by line 6 below. Desdemona must be destroyed, not from personal vengeance, but because she represents a pernicious principle which, if suffered, will corrupt all mankind.

V.ii.5. *alablaster.* Alabaster, a beautiful white stone used for the finest funeral monuments.

V.ii.12. *Promethean heat.* Prometheus, in classical mythology, stole from heaven the sacred element of fire, originally unobtainable on the earth. Othello means here that the spark of life, once extinguished, cannot be rekindled without some superhuman agency.

V.ii.16. *doth.* The Folio has 'dost,' less felicitously. Othello is commenting on the breath; he is not addressing or personifying it as the Cavalier poets did.

V.ii.20. *fatal.* Referring to Desdemona's deadliness. Cf. line 6.

V.ii.55. *conception.* The Quarto has 'conceit,' which blurs the terrible figure that Othello uses. His strong purpose is like an unwanted infant ineluctably approaching birth.

V.ii.70. *That he hath—* Othello is unable to go on, but the Folio editor was, replacing the oath *uds death* by 'vs'd thee.'

V.ii.82. *Being . . . pause.* While it is being done, there must be no pause. This is not in the Quarto and would not be missed. Perhaps an editor was working Othello's broken prose into the rhythmical pattern.

V.ii.93. *The noise was high.* Probably referring to the outcry resulting from the attack on Cassio. Othello is accounting to himself for Emilia's disturbing presence outside.

V.ii.101. *yawn at alteration.* Crack open at this monstrous change. Earthquakes were believed to accompany or follow eclipses. These lines, 97–101, recall Othello's earlier saying, III.iii.91,92.

V.ii.170. *Gra.* The Quarto gives this speech to 'All,' which was probably Shakespeare's careless indication. The Folio editor, not caring for a chorus, decided who was to speak it. He properly left 'All' in line 185.

V.ii.191. *I thought so then.* That is, at IV.ii.131 ff. (but without suspicion then of Iago's guilt).

V.ii.196. *Perchance, Iago, I will ne'er go home.* A line of great poignancy, for Emilia and Iago are fond of each other.

V.ii.216. This statement is inconsistent with III.iv.55,56, though perhaps reconcilable by casuistry. See note on III.iv.76.

V.ii.219. *No, I will speak as liberal as the north.* So the Folio. The Quarto has 'I'll be in speaking liberal as the air,' which is also good. Shakespearean revision is possible.

V.ii.233. *wife.* The Quarto has 'woman.' *no stones in heaven, etc.* Are there no extra thunderbolts to destroy creatures like Iago?

V.ii.288. *I bleed, sir.* Coldbloodedly ironic. You have drawn blood from me, as you couldn't from a real devil. This accounts for *demi-devil* in line 301.

V.ii.303. *Demand me nothing.* Iago, when caught, has been willing to confess facts (lines 296,321); but when questioned

about motives, he takes refuge in sullen silence, for he has no
answer that makes any possible sense to him.

V.ii.317. *nick.* So the first Quarto. The Folio editor found the
word inelegant and substituted 'interim,' in which perversion
he has been followed by all later editions.

V.ii.342. *Speak of them as they are.* This, the first Quarto reading, is more in character than the Folio's 'Speak of me as I am.'

V.ii.347. *Like the base Indian.* There is no significance in the
first Folio spelling, 'Iudean.' Shakespeare is thinking of the
savage who throws away a king's ransom because he cannot
realize its value. In his mind, probably, were the lines near the
beginning of Marlowe's *Jew of Malta:*

> 'Give me the merchants of the Indian mines . . .
> The wealthy Moor that in the eastern rocks
> Without control can pick his riches up,
> And in his house heap pearl like pebble-stones.'

V.ii.351. *med'cinable.* Shakespeare seems to prefer this word, with
the accent indicated, to 'medicinal,' which is the Quarto reading.

V.ii.351. *Aleppo.* Aleppo was an important center of English
oriental trade. Shakespeare was evidently interested in it; cf.
Macbeth I.iii.7. A consulate was established there in 1586,
'which became a convenient hospice and sometimes a place of
refuge for English travellers.' Shakespeare may have read William Parry's *A New and Large Discourse of the Travels of
Sir A. Sherley, etc.,* 1601. Of one of Parry's fellow travellers,
George Manwaring, it is recorded that at Aleppo 'a Turk took
him by the ear and marched him up and down the street while
the bystanders threw stones at him and spat upon him' (S. C.
Chew, *The Crescent and the Rose,* pp. 157, 245–246). For
more detail see *The Three Brothers, or the Travels and Adventures of Sir Anthony, Sir Robert, & Sir Thomas Sherley,*
1825, p. 35.

V.ii.365. *Let it be hid.* The rear-stage curtain is drawn so that the
corpses may rise and walk away. The main stage was not cur-
tained.

APPENDIX A

FURNESS cites two actual historical personages who have been named as possible models for Shakespeare's Othello. (1) Christopher Moro, a heroic Venetian general, returned to Venice in 1508 from the lord-lieutenancy of Cyprus, after the failure of 'an hypothetical' or threatened Turkish attack on the island, in mourning for his recently deceased wife. (2) San Pietro di Bastelica, an Italian adventurer of great distinction in the service of France, in 1563 returned abruptly from a mission to Constantinople (to beg assistance for the Corsicans from the Turks) because of artfully circulated reports of his innocent wife's infidelity; thereupon, after a scene of mingled tenderness and ferocity on his part and gentle submission on hers, he asked pardon upon his knees for the deed he was about to commit and then deliberately strangled her with her handkerchief. The stories of both these personages may well have been retailed in England within Shakespeare's hearing and so may have influenced him; but the chief accepted source for the play remains a prose tale by Cinthio.

Giovanbattista Giraldi, called Cinthio, was a sixteenth-century novelist, poet, dramatist, and university professor of Ferrara who compiled, and published at Monteregale, Sicily, in 1565, an edifying 'philosophical' work wherein ten moral virtues or their opposites are illustrated by ten

appropriate tales apiece,—thence entitled *Hecatommithi*
(*The Hundred Fables*). The seventh novel of the third
decade is the source of *Othello;* but Shakespeare, unless
we credit him with a knowledge of Italian or French (a
French translation appeared in 1583) or Spanish (a Spanish translation appeared in 1590), seemingly gained his
acquaintance with the *Hecatommithi* at second hand, for
no English translation of the work in the sixteenth or
seventeenth centuries is known to us.

Cinthio gives a name to none of his prototypes of
Shakespeare's characters except the heroine, who is called
'Disdemona.' Othello is simply 'the Moor,' Iago 'the Ensign,' Cassio 'the Captain of the troop' or 'the Captain,'
Emilia 'the Ensign's wife,' and Bianca 'a courtesan,' while
Brabantio, Lodovico, Gratiano, Montano, Roderigo, the
Duke, and the Clown do not appear, and on the other
hand 'the Captain of the troop' is provided with an un-
named wife. Cinthio's narrative may be summarized thus,
for the sake of the instructive lesson it affords in Shakespeare's method of plot-construction:—

Despite parental opposition, Disdemona loved and married a valiant Moor who had rendered distinguished military service to the Venetian state, and the two lived happily together in Venice for some time, till the Senate
appointed the Moor to the command of the troops being
sent out as a new garrison for Cyprus. Rather than be
separated from her husband, Disdemona insisted upon
sharing the perils of the voyage. They accordingly set sail
and in due time 'with a perfectly tranquil sea arrived
safely at Cyprus.'[1] Now a wicked Ensign among the

[1] The quotations are taken from Taylor's translation, 1855, as
reprinted by Furness.

soldiery, of whose wife Disdemona became very fond, fell passionately in love with the Moor's wife and 'bent all his thoughts to achieve his conquest; . . . but she, whose every wish was centred in the Moor, had no thought for this Ensign more than for any other man.' The Ensign, ascribing his failure to a certain Captain of a troop to whom Disdemona had always shown great kindness, because of the Moor's affection for him, determined to revenge himself by bringing about the death of the Captain and destroying the Moor's love for the lady. 'Not long afterwards it happened that the Captain, having drawn his sword upon a soldier of the guard, and struck him,' was punished by being deprived of his rank; Disdemona's impulsive intercession thereupon, out of mere friendliness and concern lest her husband should 'lose so dear a friend,' gave the wicked Ensign a hint upon which he promptly acted by dexterously insinuating to the Moor, 'after feigning at first great reluctance to say aught that might displease,' that the lady sought the Captain's restoration to favor for her own sake, 'and all the more since she has taken an aversion to your blackness.' The enraged husband's demand for positive proof was temporarily satisfied by lies and promises, and afterwards 'the villain resolved on a new deed of guilt.

'Disdemona often used to go to visit the Ensign's wife, and remained with her a good part of the day. Now the Ensign observed that she carried about with her a handkerchief, which he knew the Moor had given her, finely embroidered in the Moorish fashion. Then he conceived the plan of taking this kerchief from her secretly, and thus laying the snare for her final ruin. The Ensign had a little daughter, a child three years of age, who was much loved

by Disdemona, and one day, when the unhappy lady had
gone to pay a visit at the house of this vile man, he took
the little child up in his arms and carried her to Disdemona, who took her and pressed her to her bosom; whilst
at the same instant this traitor, who had extreme dexterity
of hand, drew the kerchief from her sash so cunningly
that she did not notice him.'

After this 'it seemed as if fate conspired with the Ensign
to work the death of the unhappy Disdemona.' The handkerchief was dropped in the Captain's apartment and
found by him; the Moor was made to witness a conversation in which the Ensign's pantomime seemed to indicate
that the Captain was confessing everything; Disdemona
naturally failed to produce the handkerchief when it was
called for; and the Moor, wholly convinced now, 'fell to
meditating how he should put his wife to death, and likewise the Captain, so that their death should not be laid to
his charge.' 'The Ensign's wife, who knew the whole
truth, but dared not, from fear of her husband, disclose a
single circumstance,' tried to warn Disdemona indirectly,
but the Ensign pointed out to the Moor the Captain's
wife 'standing at a window, where she could be seen by
all the passers-by in the street,' with the handkerchief in
her possession, and the doom of the two innocent victims
was sealed. 'After much entreating and being richly paid,'
the Ensign finally overcame his fears and one dark night
assaulted the Captain, who was 'on his way to visit a
courtesan,' and with one blow cut off his right leg at the
thigh; only the wounded man's vigorous sword-play and
the speedy response to his cries for assistance saved his life.

Then the Ensign and the Moor 'consulted of one means
and another—poison and daggers—to kill poor Disdemona,

but could resolve on nothing. At length the Ensign said, "A plan comes to my mind, which will give you satisfaction and raise cause for no suspicion. It is this: the house in which you live is very old, and the ceiling of your chamber has many cracks; I propose we take a stocking filled with sand, and beat Disdemona with it till she dies; thus will her body bear no signs of violence. When she is dead we can pull down a portion of the ceiling, and thus make it seem as if a rafter falling on her head had killed the lady. Suspicion cannot rest on you, since all men will impute her death to accident." This cruel counsel pleased the Moor, and he only waited for a fitting time to execute the plot. One night, when he and Disdemona had retired to bed, the Ensign, whom the Moor had concealed in a closet which opened into the chamber, raised a noise in the closet, according to a concerted plan; whereat the Moor said to his wife, "Did you not hear that noise?"

'"Indeed I heard it," she replied.

'"Rise," said the Moor, "and see what 'tis."

'The unhappy Disdemona rose from bed, and the instant she approached the closet, out rushed the Ensign, and being strong and of stout nerve, he beat her cruelly with the bag of sand across her back; upon which Disdemona fell to the ground, scarce able to draw her breath; but with the little voice she had left, she called upon the Moor for aid. But the Moor, leaping from bed, exclaimed, "Thou wickedest of women, thus has thy falseness found its just reward." . . . The wretched lady, hearing these words, and feeling that she was near her end (for the Ensign had given her another blow), appealed to the justice of Heaven, since justice here had failed her, in proof of her fidelity and truth; and as she was thus calling Heaven to witness, the wicked Ensign inflicted a third blow, under which she sank lifeless on the floor. Then the Ensign and the Moor, laying Disdemona on the bed and wounding her head, pulled down part of the ceiling of the chamber as they had arranged; whereupon the Moor began to call aloud for help, exclaiming that the house was falling. Hearing this uproar, the neighbors all came running up, and there found Disdemona lying dead beneath a rafter,— a sight which, from the good life of that poor lady, did fill all hearts with sorrow.'

The two murderers escaped detection for the time being, but remorse finally caused the Moor so to hate his accomplice that, kept from slaying him by fear of consequences, he deprived him of his rank and dismissed him. In revenge the Ensign told the Captain, now going about on a wooden leg, that it was the Moor who had cut off his leg and killed Disdemona. They both repeated these charges before the Senate; and the Moor was thereupon brought pinioned to Venice, tortured, imprisoned, and 'condemned to perpetual banishment, in which he was eventually slain by the kinsfolk of Disdemona, as he merited. The Ensign returned to his own country, and following up his wonted villainy,' lodged a false accusation against a companion, for which he was tortured so violently to make him prove his charges that 'his body ruptured' and 'he died a miserable death. Thus did Heaven avenge the innocence of Disdemona.'

APPENDIX B

THE HISTORY OF THE PLAY

ON the strength of Malone's assertion, backed by a now generally credited reference in the Revels Books,[1] the composition of *Othello* is assigned to the year 1604; but no printed version is known to have appeared for eighteen years after that time, until the First Quarto was published by Thomas Walkley, in 1622, having been licensed 6 October 1621. This is the latest in date of all Shakespearean quarto first editions of single plays before the appearance of the famous collected edition of the plays by Heminge and Condell, known as the First Folio, in 1623; and indeed Walkley's advance knowledge of the forthcoming folio publication probably accounts for this quarto issue as an attempt to make something out of his single holding while there was yet time.

Richard Burbage, the leading tragedian of Shakespeare's company, won great fame in the rôle of Othello, as attested by tributes in verse upon his death in 1619. The title-page of the First Quarto assures us that the play had 'beene diuerse times acted at the Globe, and at the Black Friers, by his Maiesties Seruants,' but the *Shakspere*

---

[1] The entry, recording the performance of the play at court, reads: 'By the King's Majesty's Players. Hallowmas Day, being the first of November [1604], a play in the banqueting house at Whitehall called *The Moor of Venice.*'

Allusion Book records only two performances between 1604 and 1622: one attended by the German Ambassador at the Globe, 30 April 1610, and the other before Prince Charles (later Charles I), his sister the Princess Elizabeth, and her fiancé the Elector Palatine, presumably at Whitehall, in 1612 or 1613. Three other performances can be definitely dated before the closing of the theatres, in 1642; viz., 22 November 1629; 6 May 1635, 'att the bla: ffryers'; and 8 December 1636, before the King and Queen at Hampton Court; but other references show that the play's popularity was far greater than these meager surviving accounts would indicate. There was a notable production at Oxford in September 1610, when *Othello* was given along with Jonson's then new comedy, *The Alchemist*, to the scandalous delight of the students. In the *Allusion Book's* 'List of Shakspere's Works, arranged according to the number of allusions to each' during the period from 1591 to 1700, *Hamlet* leads with 95 references, and *Othello* stands fifth with 56.[1]

The modern era on the English stage begins with the reopening of the theatres at the Restoration, when actresses and painted scenery were first introduced as regular features of public performances. Here *Othello* figures conspicuously, for on the eighth of December 1660, at the Red Bull, the first woman to appear on the public stage in England played the part of Desdemona. The experiment was undertaken with some misgivings, as Jordan's defensive prologue shows:

[1] G. E. Bentley, *Shakespeare and Jonson: their Reputations in the Seventeenth Century Compared*, p. 109, places *Othello* second only to *The Tempest* among Shakespeare's works in seventeenth-century reputation.

In this reforming age
We have intents to civilize the Stage.
Our 'women' are defective, and so siz'd
You'd think they were some of the Guard disguiz'd;
For (to speak truth) men act, that are between
Forty and fifty, Wenches of fifteen;
With bone so large, and nerve so incomplyant,
When you call *Desdemona,* enter Giant.

As might be expected, Pepys has some interesting remarks on Restoration performances of *Othello:* '1660, October 11.—To the Cockpitt to see "The Moore of Venice," which was well done. Burt acted the Moore; by the same token, a very pretty lady that sat by me, called out, to see Desdemona smothered.' '1669, February 6.—To the King's playhouse, and there in an upper box . . . did see "The Moor of Venice": but ill acted in most parts; Mohun, which did a little surprise me, not acting Iago's part by much so well as Clun used to do: nor another, Hart's[1] which was Cassio's; nor indeed, Burt doing the Moor's so well as I once thought he did.' These actors belonged to Sir William Davenant's[2] Drury Lane company; in one cast in 1663, with the above named, Cartwright, a great Falstaff, played Brabantio and Mrs. Hughes Desdemona. *Othello* remained a particular favorite throughout the Restoration and Queen Anne periods, largely owing to the genius of the great Thomas Betterton (1635?–1710). Steele's tribute in the *Tatler* to Betterton's 'wonderful agony' in the last three acts, is familiar, and Colley Cibber's summary often quoted: 'Betterton was an actor as Shakespeare was an author, both without competitors,

[1] Shakespeare's grandnephew.
[2] Shakespeare's godson (?).

formed for the mutual assistance and illustration of each other's genius' (Genest I, 492). Genest's record shows that *Othello* was produced practically every season during the period covered, 1660–1830, and, what is more significant still, produced in its original form, when almost every other Shakespearean or Elizabethan play was presented only in some mutilated 'adaptation' or 'revision.'

Betterton's mantle descended upon Barton Booth (1681–1733), whose Othello was considered by Colley Cibber his best rôle. Like Betterton, he probably played the part in the court-dress of the period. His successor, Quin, who dominated the stage till Garrick's triumphal entry in 1741, appeared in an English military uniform, a large powdered wig, and white gloves; when the latter were removed, the sudden disclosure of his blackened hands made emphatic Othello's alien race. David Garrick (1717–1779) made one of his few failures when he attempted the rôle of Othello, in spite of his great success as Hamlet, Macbeth, and Lear, and wisely avoided the part. Barry's splendid impersonation of the Moor, and Macklin's and Henderson's of Iago, save the credit of the performances of this period. Even Kemble failed to costume Othello properly, while his wonderful sister, Mrs. Siddons, was a far better Lady Macbeth than Desdemona. Edmund Kean won from all critics the most complete and superlative approval ever accorded any interpreter of Othello's part. The descriptions of his performance make one wonder at the change that has come over actors (or audiences?) in our own time. As is well known, Kean fell stricken upon the shoulder of his son Charles (playing Iago) during what was to have been his farewell appearance at Covent Garden, 25 March 1833, and died a few weeks later. He was the first to present Othello as a light brown or bronzed Moor instead of as a jet-black negro; and he was also a very fine Iago. Junius Brutus Booth played Iago to Kean's Othello in a notable competitive performance at Drury Lane, 20 February 1817, and later, chiefly in America, created an interesting if not wholly convincing interpretation of the Moor as a case of Oriental racial characteristics slowly overcoming an artificial Christian civilization. William C. Macready (1793–1873), who was the first to costume Othello with complete correctness, was really greater as Iago. Sir Henry Irving's first appearance as Othello, 14 February 1876, at the London 'Lyceum,' was too untrammeled by tradition to be appreciated; but on 2 May 1881, he began a brilliantly successful engagement at the 'Lyceum' with Edwin Booth, the two actors alternating the rôles of Othello and Iago at successive performances, to the Desdemona of Ellen Terry, the Cassio of William Terriss, and the Roderigo of Arthur Wing Pinero. Booth's Othello far surpassed Irving's, but the two were perhaps evenly matched as Iago. The famous Italian actor, Tommaso Salvini, was also thrilling audiences in Europe and America in the '70's and '80's by the almost animal passionateness of his interpretation of Othello's jealousy. Sir Johnston Forbes-Robertson essayed Othello in 1898, and again, with Gertrude Elliott as Desdemona, in May 1913; but his Othello was inferior to his Hamlet. Sir Herbert Beerbohm Tree produced *Othello* in London, in April 1912, with his usual scenic elaboration, Laurence Irving playing the part of Iago and Phyllis Neilson-Terry that of Desdemona.

America may claim at least two very great performers of the two rôles (for most great Othellos have also been great Iagos), in Edwin Forrest (1806–1872) and Edwin Booth (1833–1893), while John Edward McCullough (1837–1885) was also successful. Richard Mansfield steadily declined to attempt the part, on the ground that he could add nothing to Salvini's performance. E. H. Sothern appeared early in his career as Roderigo in one of McCullough's last performances, and William Faversham gave a deserving but unsuccessful performance in 1913. The most impressive recent production was that of the New York Theatre Guild (1943), directed by Margaret Webster, with Paul Robeson as Othello and Jose Ferrer as Iago.

Index of Words Glossed

Figures in full-faced type indicate page-numbers